PORTRAIT OF A WESTMEATH TENANT
COMMUNITY 1879–85
The Barbavilla Murder

Maynooth Studies in Local History

GENERAL EDITOR   Raymond Gillespie

This pamphlet is one of eight new additions to the Maynooth Studies in Local History series in 1999. Like their twenty predecessors, most are based on theses submitted for the M.A. in Local History at National University of Ireland, Maynooth. The pamphlets are not concerned primarily with the portrayal of the history of 'particular places'. All are local in their focus but that localisation is determined not by administrative boundaries but rather the limits of the experience of everyday life in the regions of Ireland over time. In some of these works the local experience is of a single individual while in others social, occupational or religious groups form the primary focus of enquiry.

The results of these enquiries into the shaping of local societies in the past emphasises, again, the diversity of the Irish historical experience. Ranging across problems of economic disaster, political transformation, rural unrest and religious tension, these works show how such problems were grounded in the realities of everyday life in local communities. The responses to such challenges varied from region to region, each place coping with problems in its own way, determined by its historical evolution and contemporary constraints.

The result of such investigations can only increase our awareness of the complexity of Ireland's historical evolution. Each work, in its own right, is also a significant contribution to our understanding of how specific Irish communities have developed in all their richness and diversity. In all, they demonstrate the vibrancy and challenging nature of local history.

Maynooth Studies in Local History: Number 25

Portrait of a Westmeath Tenant Community 1879–85

The Barbavilla Murder

Ann Murtagh

IRISH ACADEMIC PRESS

DUBLIN • PORTLAND, OR

First published in 1999 by
IRISH ACADEMIC PRESS
44, Northumberland Road, Dublin 4, Ireland
and in the United States of America by
IRISH ACADEMIC PRESS
c/o ISBS, 5804 NE Hassalo Street, Portland, OR 97213.

website: www.iap.ie

British Library Cataloguing in Publication Data
Murtagh, Ann
    Portrait of a Westmeath Tenant Community, 1879–85: the Barbavilla Murder
    (Maynooth studies in local history; 25)
    1. Murder – Ireland –Westmeath (County) – History – 19th century 2.Violence –
    Ireland – Westmeath (County) – History – 19th century 3. Landlord and tenant
    – Ireland – Westmeath (County) – History – 19th century
    I. Title
    364. 1'523'0941815

Library of Congress Cataloging-in-Publication Data
Murtagh, Ann.
        Portrait of a Westmeath Tenant Community, 1879–85: The Barbavilla Murder/
    Ann Murtagh.
            p.   cm. — (Maynooth studies in local history; no. 25)
        Includes bibliographical references and index.
        ISBN 0–7165–2673–5 (pbk.).
        1. Murder—Ireland—Westmeath—History—19th century Case studies.
    2. Peasants uprisings—Ireland—History—19th century. 3. Land tenure—Ireland
    —History—19th century. I. Title. II. Series.
        HV6535.I743W475   1999
        364. 15'23'0941815—dc21   99–29356
                                                                              CIP

Typeset in 10 pt on 12 pt Bembo by
Carrigboy Typesetting Services, County Cork
Printed by ColourBooks Ltd, Dublin

Contents

Preface

I am indebted to a number of people from the Collinstown area on whose local knowledge and expertise I drew while researching this study: Micheál Conlon, Cáit Monaghan, Chrissie Byrne, Tommy and Jane Daly and the late Paddy Tuite. In particular, I wish to express my gratitude to Billy Smyth for access to the Smyth of Drumcree papers, and to Phil Tierney of Mullingar, who kindly provided the postcard of Barbavilla House.

My thanks to the staffs of the various libraries, especially the National Library of Ireland; Westmeath County Library, Mullingar; Meath County Library, Navan; and particularly Tom Quinlan of the National Archives, Dublin. The assistance of Professor Vincent Comerford, N.U.I. Maynooth, Dr. Patrick Maume, The Queen's University, Belfast, and Kevin Mulligan, Kells, is also acknowledged. Sincere thanks to Dr. Enda Delaney, my M.A. supervisor, for his professional guidance and encouragement, and to Dr. Carla King for her input at the earlier stages of this study. To my classmates of 1996–8 and our tutors Dr. Raymond Gillespie and Dr. Mary Ann Lyons, I wish to express my gratitude for their stimulating and valued company. Finally, I would like to acknowledge the tremendous support that I have received from my family and to dedicate this work to the memory of my father, Joe Murtagh, who passed away before its completion.

Introduction

The Roman Catholic parish of St Mary's, Collinstown, nestles among the hills and lakes of north Westmeath. In terms of soil fertility, like the county itself, it is an area of contrasts with large tracts of fertile land interspersed with areas of poorer quality soil. Griffith's valuation (1854) is useful in providing an overview of the quality of the soil in the mid-nineteenth century and this source indicates that the southern area of the parish was the more fertile part.[1] By the 1870s this area was characterised by a group of three demesnes, each with a resident landowner: Drumcree (4,431 acres), Barbavilla (2,108 acres) and Ralphsdale or Glananea (1,256 acres).[2] The owners of each of these estates had descended from Bishop William Smyth who had purchased land in Westmeath in 1670.[3] The village of Collinstown was sustained in economic terms by the Barbavilla estate, while the other two estates supported the village of Drumcree.

The Catholic parish of St Mary's, Collinstown, is the geographical unit chosen for this study. It consists of four civil parishes: Collinstown, Fore, Kilcumny and Kilpatrick, and had two churches, St Mary's in Collinstown and St Feighin's in Fore. On account of the strong identification which tenants had with the parish to which they belonged, the Catholic parish was deemed to be the most appropriate unit to study this tenant community. The fact that the local branch of the Land League founded in 1880 was the 'Collinstown and Fore' branch, referring to the two half parishes which combined to make the unit of the parish of Collinstown, demonstrates the contemporary relevance of this unit. Within the boundaries of the Catholic parish were two Church of Ireland churches, St Feighin's in Collinstown, (built in 1843) and St John's in Drumcree, (built in 1811).[4] According to the 1881 census, 9 per cent of the population living within the boundaries of the Catholic parish of Collinstown was Protestant.[5] Although the parish unit forms the basis for this study, reference is frequently made to the Poor Law Union of Delvin in which the parish is situated and to the larger administrative unit of the county of Westmeath itself. Thus these larger units provide the context for the study and, as Phythian-Adams recommends, there is a deliberate attempt, not to be too tightly focused inwards, but instead to look 'outwards and relationally'.[6] With this in mind, the principal objective of this study is to examine a murder which took place within the context of the tenant community who lived in this parish between the years 1879–85. This in turn is appraised in the context of landlord-tenant relations in County Westmeath in order to provide a relevant regional backdrop for the study of this community. While the focus is undoubtedly a

7

local one, events in Collinstown are placed firmly within the broader framework of the history of the Irish land question. This link with the wider picture is essential in order to provide an adequate analysis of the events in the parish and county before and after the murder. The sources were examined to evaluate the origins of the long-term tensions which may explain the murder and how this event in turn affected the community in a number of ways. It was found, for instance, that there was a history of conflict between a local landlord and the Catholic clergy dating from at least the 1830s. It seems appropriate therefore that two of the main printed sources consulted were written by this landlord, William Barlow Smythe, and the Roman Catholic parish priest in Collinstown, Rev. John Curry.

Smythe was the intended victim of the shooting in April 1882, which killed his sister-in-law, Maria Smythe. Within three weeks of the murder he published a pamphlet in Britain, *The tale of Westmeath, wickedness and woe* (1882). According to Smythe, he had been 'asked to circulate, in a compendious form, documents – some already published – connected with this horrible event'.[7] The unwitting testimony contained in this pamphlet is crucial to an understanding of the tensions which existed in Collinstown before the murder. The bias of this document is an important consideration, as the basis on which it came into existence was to publicise the injustice of the events surrounding the murder and the evils of the land agitation from Smythe's point of view. With this proviso in mind, it is nevertheless a valuable source for studying landlord-tenant relations in Collinstown before and immediately after the murder. *The Barbavilla trials and the crimes act in Ireland* (1886) is the title of the second pamphlet dealing with the murder.[8] Like the *Tale*, this pamphlet contains a strong bias, since it is imbued with a strong Irish nationalist tone. In some senses therefore, these two sources complement each other. Rev. John Curry first published this pamphlet in 1885 in order to highlight the case of the Barbavilla prisoners, eleven men he believed were wrongly convicted for the conspiracy of the Barbavilla murder. The main body of the text consists of extracts from the court proceedings and Curry's examination of the evidence, the character of the crown witnesses and the alleged irregularities regarding the role of local policemen in the case. In the absence of court transcripts, this is a particularly useful source as depositions, for example, are included in their entirety.[9] It contains a wealth of source material which brings to life the world in which the tenant community lived during the 1880s, albeit from the standpoint which was sympathetic to the plight of the tenants.

However as valuable as these two sources have proven to be, the complexities of researching a murder demanded that an extensive range of other source material should be examined. This material ranged from official papers of the chief secretary's office and contemporary newspapers, both national and provincial, to the private papers of the Barbavilla and Drumcree estates and tape-recorded oral testimony. The bulk of the Smythe of Barbavilla papers are found in the National Library of Ireland where to date they have undergone only a preliminary sorting. A smaller, yet useful collection, is housed in the Westmeath County Library in Mullingar. The third body for estate papers is the Smyth of Drumcree collection which is in private hands. Local newspapers were found to be invaluable to this study. In addition to providing an abundance of factual information, their editorial predilections reveal the political outlook, attitudes and assumptions of their intended readership.

As in the case of the pamphlets by Curry and Smythe, there were two opposing points of view represented in the newspapers in Westmeath. The *Westmeath Guardian* founded by the Kidd family in 1835 was well known as the establishment paper of the midlands. It epitomised the Protestant, pro-landlord perspective; Smythe's letters frequently are found among its columns, which further enhances this newspaper as a source. In 1882 the pro-nationalist *Westmeath Examiner* was launched in response to a demand for a newspaper which would represent the interests of a large sector of the population in Westmeath who were effectively ignored by the existing county paper. Thus having two local newspapers which contrasted in their political affiliation allows for a more analytical assessment of the reporting of an event.

The coverage of the land war of 1879–82 contained in these newspapers is of particular significance for this study. It is a period in the county's history that has been for the most part neglected by historians. The Westmeath outrages of 1869–71 have attracted considerable attention from scholars such as Vaughan, Murray, Townshend and Crossman.[10] Likewise, the anti-grazier movement in Meath and Westmeath in the early twentieth century has formed an important element of Jones's study of the grazier community.[11] Therefore, this present study contributes to the existing state of knowledge of the land war in Westmeath. It also demonstrates that the problems associated with the practices of graziers mainly in relation to competition for land which underscored the period of unrest of 1869–71 and the anti-grazier movement of the early twentieth century, were also an important feature of the land war in Westmeath.

Westmeath was an area which was traditionally associated with agrarian violence, and therefore an important theme of this study is this tradition of agrarian violence and unrest. Why did people resort to violence? Various facets of the tenant community are examined in order to address this question, such as changes in the rural economy by local figures and participation by local figures in the Land League agitation in the early 1880s. Moreover, agrarian violence is interconnected with another theme: the relations within the tenant community. The demands of the agricultural economy, for instance, had an important bearing on the relations between the smaller tenants and graziers concerning the available land resources. Finally, the relations between the landlord and tenant community in Collinstown are examined, in particular the response of each group to the Land League agitation of the early 1880s.

The first section provides the necessary context for this study by examining the concept of agrarian violence and its connection with changes in agricultural economy between the Famine (1845–50) and the land war (1879–82) in County Westmeath. It also examines processes which were important external influences on the tenants in Collinstown, such as the increased access to education and the commercialisation of agriculture. In addition, the limited access of the tenant community to the political process is considered here. The second part discusses the impact of the agricultural depression in the area and the participation of the tenants, both male and female, in the Land League movement of the late 1870s and early 1880s. Also of concern here is a local landlord, William Barlow Smythe (1809–89) and the pivotal role he played in the events which unfolded. The eviction and murder and the response to these events by various communities of interest such as the tenants, the press, the churches and the government are the central focus of the third section. The final part of this study looks at the tenant community in the aftermath of the murder. It also examines the police investigation, the arrests and the subsequent trials from a number of perspectives including the nature of support the prisoners received from the local community. The efforts of Rev. John Curry, the Roman Catholic parish priest of Collinstown, to have the case reopened and the factors which influenced the outcome of his campaign are also appraised. This study deals with the alleged connection between this murder and the Invincibles, the secret society which was responsible for the assassination of chief secretary, Lord Cavendish, and under-secretary, T.H. Burke in May, 1882, usually referred to as the Phoenix Park murders.

In conclusion, this study examines a murder in the context of a local tenant community, which in turn is evaluated in reference to landlord-tenant relations in Westmeath and the broader context of the Irish land question. It seeks to discuss underlying causes of agrarian violence in Westmeath during the land war 1879–82, linking it with earlier agrarian violence which characterised the years 1869–71. Moreover, by appraising the complexities associated with the Barbavilla Murder, this study contributes to the existing state of knowledge of the land question and ultimately to a greater understanding of the dynamics of the land war at local level.

Between the Famine and the Land War, 1850–79

To set the scene, it is important to examine the theme of agrarian violence in County Westmeath, in particular the outbreak which occurred between the years 1869 and 1871. The sources generated by this upsurge in agrarian violence – attributed by the authorities to 'Ribbonism' – provide many useful insights into tensions which existed in the community in Collinstown and indeed County Westmeath before the land war. Fundamental to such an analysis of agrarian crime is an appraisal of the changes which were taking place in the agricultural economy at the time. As Gillespie and Moran have pointed out, economic changes could bring about new tensions in the community, and the agrarian violence which characterised the years between 1869 and 1871 in Westmeath, were to a large extent a symptom of the expansion of grazing in the area, itself a result of the increasing commercialisation of Irish agricultural production.[1] The association between Ribbonism and County Westmeath was a strong and enduring one, and a persistent thorn in the side of government officials from at least 1815 onwards. There is abundant evidence to support the existence of this long association in a varied range of sources, including parliamentary papers, police files and contemporary newspapers. Defining exactly what is meant by Ribbonism is by far a more difficult and exacting task. In pre-Famine Ireland, Ribbonmen were one of the many rural, oath-bound, secret societies which were proscribed by the government. Their violence was motivated by economic considerations, but it was economics, as Townshend notes 'with a strong ethical foundation'.[2] It was mainly in defence of labourers' interests that these crimes were perpetrated against larger farmers. There is contemporary evidence which suggests that Ribbonism spread from Cavan and Longford to north Westmeath in 1830.[3] Although the effects of the great Irish Famine significantly reduced the number of labourers in the county, Westmeath continued to be identified with Ribbonism during sporadic waves of rural disturbance in the 1860s and 1870s. However, it was the outbreak of agrarian violence during the years 1869–71 which once again resulted in Westmeath being declared as 'the centre of a hot-bed of Ribbonism'.[4] Local government officials clamoured for the suspension of *habeas corpus*, which would allow for the detention of suspects without trial, in the belief that this was the only effective method of restoring peace and order. In order to ascertain that such a step was necessary the cabinet established a parliamentary inquiry in March 1871 to examine the evidence of Ribbonism in County Westmeath.

Several witnesses testified before this select committee, providing accounts of an organised, sophisticated secret society with political motives, operating within an extensive network.[5]

The belief in the existence of a formidable confederacy displayed by the witnesses in question, was the typical reaction of police and magistrates at the time. Since the mid-nineteenth century serious agrarian crime had come to be identified by these officials as 'Ribbonism'. Indeed, the belief in the existence of the pre-Famine Ribbon society persisted among those investigating agrarian crime in Ireland until the late nineteenth century.[6] The evidence, however, on which this evaluation was based was mainly circumstantial. Attributing agrarian crime to Ribbonmen and therefore classifying it as political, became an accepted practice which was never seriously questioned by those in charge of law and order. Nulty, who also gave evidence before the committee argued that the agrarian violence in Westmeath was not of a political nature. On the basis of information gathered from the Catholic clergy throughout the county in the spring of 1871, he stated that the perpetrators of the recent crimes were more likely members of 'little cliques' which had 'no union subsisting between them except, perhaps, a sort of sympathy in a bad cause'.[7] The most thorough scholarly study on the subject of Ribbonism likewise concludes that there was insufficient evidence to establish the fact of a 'great confederacy directed against landlords'.[8] Murray examined the 'myth of Ribbonism' in Westmeath during this period and argues that the term 'Ribbonism' came to be used as a label 'affixed by the police and magistrates to crimes they could not solve, criminals they could not catch, and gangs they could not break up'.[9] This would seem a plausible explanation given the embarrassingly large number of unsolved crimes, among them six homicides, which characterised the period 1869–71. The alleged existence of a Ribbon society provided a credible and face-saving façade, behind which the police and magistrates could conceal their extreme difficulty in identifying the culprits. It also strengthened the case, as far as the local government officials were concerned at least, for the local suspension of *habeas corpus*.[10] Notwithstanding the obvious difficulty in interpreting the term Ribbonism, there is no doubt that Westmeath experienced a serious breakdown of law and order during the years 1869–71, as is clearly borne out by an analysis of the crime statistics. Between July 1869 and February 1871, 327 agrarian offences were reported in the county as opposed to 235 for the complete period 1862–68.[11] What was the purpose of those who engaged in agrarian violence and what precipitated this increase? It seems likely that it was perpetrated in defence of a customary, unwritten agrarian code, as one Englishman, George Campbell, commented in 1869: 'In Ireland there are two sets of laws – the English . . . and the laws and customs of the country'.[12] This code reflected the interests of small farmers and labourers and had to be defended not alone against 'predatory' landlords, but also larger tenants. Threatening letters which abounded during these years, frequently refer to this alternative set of laws. 'There are Irish laws at present which will be carried out efficiently', one writer in the Collinstown area declared to a local landlord.[13] The 'traditional code' frowned upon unjust rents, evictions, the taking of a holding from which another tenant had been evicted, and the erosion of certain traditional privileges. An important aspect of this code was the effect of the threat of violence. Threats were taken seriously with good reason, owing to the strong possibility of their implementation should they be ignored. The threat of violence had a regulatory effect on people's behaviour, which, as Townshend points out, is akin to the effect of 'what is ordinarily described as law'.[14] The irony is that individuals or small groups who resorted to violence to protect their rights, did so in an attempt to maintain the status quo, not – as was often interpreted by government officials – to bring about revolutionary change. Therefore, the self-appointed 'upholders' of the traditional code were conservative in their outlook, rather than radical.

What was happening in County Westmeath between the years 1869 and 1871 which threatened the traditional code thereby causing this upsurge in agrarian crime? According to Vaughan, an economic explanation for the agrarian violence asserts that the profits of grazing land had reached a peak in the season 1868–9 and possibly intensified the fierce competition for any land which was available in the following year.[15] The sources relating to the parish of Collinstown and the neighbouring area for this period indicate that the prevalence of grazing was a major factor in this rural unrest. A threatening notice posted on the market house in Collinstown village in February 1869 illustrates the tension which existed in the area over the competition for land.

NOTICE TO THE PUBLIC

> We do hereby warn all landsharks not to take or have anything to do whatsoever with house or land from which a tenant is evicted. We also warn those landjobbers who are in the habit of taking large tracts of grazing land from year to year that was let to the public heretofore, that they must give it up, as these lands must be let for the use of the public as formerly – and any tyrant landlord who turns out a tenant will meet with his reward – any person who acts contrary to this notice will be shot.

ENEMIES TO OPPRESSION[16]

The 'landjobbers ' addressed in the notice were local 'graziers' or 'ranchers'. Jones has defined ranching as being 'exclusively a commercial activity involving the grazing of large numbers of sheep and dry cattle over extensive ranges of grassland'.[17] The reference in the above notice to the 'taking of large tracts of grazing land taken from year to year' refers to the 'eleven-month system', which became particularly common after 1870. This involved land being auctioned with the highest bidder securing its use for eleven months, after which time it went up for auction again. There was no formal tenancy involved, or indeed legal interest, as land had to be held on a yearly or leasehold basis to qualify for such a contract or agreement.[18] Crotty in his discussion of land tenure draws attention to the fact that graziers could operate with reasonable efficiency once they were guaranteed the possession of pasture for the grazing season, or at least a portion of it.[19] Therefore long-term security of tenure would not be as important a concern for graziers as it would be for tillage farmers, for instance. Given the relatively low margins per head in dry cattle grazing, extensive holdings were required for ranching. In order to meet this need, graziers, in most cases, held multiple holdings, which were parcelled out in different locations, and which were often left in the supervision of herdsmen. In fact, it was extremely rare for a grazier's land to be all in one holding.[20] Landlords occasionally converted common grazing land to eleven-month letting, as had happened in Collinstown – indicated by the threatening notice on the market house – and this further intensified the antagonism towards the graziers. Cottiers resented the reduced availability of land for conacre brought about by this system, and tenants of small holdings of five to fifteen acres, who were involved in the rearing of calves and young stores, were unable to compete with graziers for extra land for pasture. In some instances graziers evicted small tenants from their property in order to acquire more land for pasture, as in the case of Ned Hope of Clondalever.[21] Consequently, an 'armed party' visited Hope on 24 April 1870 with the object of 'persuading' him to give up land.[22] It seemed that Hope did not acquiesce with this suggestion. He duly reported the crime, but no charges were ever made.

The labour extensive nature of ranching was a cause of concern among the labourers and cottiers seeking employment in the area. According to a pamphlet published in Mullingar in 1873 '. . . to such extremes do some of the Bullockocrasy carry their anti-employment ideas, that they refuse to employ a married herd lest the wife and children should get sustenance on their property'.[23] The situation in Collinstown parish was exacerbated by the numerical predominance of small holders and cottiers, many of whom depended on agricultural employment outside their own holding.

Given the speculative, capitalistic and highly competitive nature of ranching, it is not surprising that it was at variance with the traditional code of landholding. However, from an economic point of view, graziers were responding to the market forces which prevailed at the time. An improvement in living standards in Britain increased the demand for livestock products from Ireland causing cattle, sheep and butter prices to rise, especially from the 1830s onwards.[24] Ireland's maritime climate was more suitable to grass growing than cereal crops which was another advantage when it came to grazing. The large fertile tracts of land in Westmeath provided high quality grazing pasture, particularly for the 'fattener ranchers' who bought young stores between the ages of 18 months and 2.5 years and fattened them for slaughter.[25] Associated with the expansion of dry cattle farming was the increased commercialisation of agriculture. This in turn extended the range of people with whom the tenant community interacted.[26] For instance, tenants in the area of study brought their livestock to a number of fairs including Collinstown, Castlepollard, Delvin, Mullingar, Oldcastle, Granard, Ballyjamesduff, Granard, Ballymahon, Edgeworthstown, Kinnegad and Killucan.[27] There they mingled with other tenants and dealers from several other places. Increased commercialisation also brought them in contact with shops and public houses. The bond between the farming community and shopkeepers became strengthened with the increase in 'shop-purchase consumption'.[28] This bond was to have important implications for the growth of the Land League in the late 1870s.

Another major development, which heralded change for the tenant community in Westmeath, was the coming of the railway in 1848. This facilitated the shipping of cattle, and also provided a means of transport for tenant farmers to travel to the fairs which were a considerable distance away. However, the degree to which dry cattle specialisation was influenced by the railway should not be exaggerated as Kennedy argues that most of the trends associated with dry cattle farming throughout Ireland were firmly in place before the coming of the railway.[29] The expanding railway network also linked rural communities with the outside world in another important way: a greater variety of goods could be shipped quickly and with relative ease into an area. Likewise, a broad cross section of people could travel to rural communities, such as commercial agents, politicians and religious leaders, bringing the tenant community within reach of worlds far beyond the confines of the parish. Furthermore, the efficiency and speed of the postal service was greatly enhanced by the railway network.[30]

The wider community of the national school system to which the tenant community had access had important implications. Access to education increased in the parish of Collinstown, and this was particularly the case in the post-Famine period. In 1868 a royal commission of inquiry into primary education was established, and its brief included a census of the number of children actually present in each primary school on 25 June 1868. Eight schools were listed in returns for the parish of Collinstown, in which 292 pupils were present.[31] The impact of increased access to education is clearly demonstrated by the census data: the number of people who could read and write in the parish rose from 45.5 per cent in 1841 to 74.6 per cent in 1881.[32] Higher levels of literacy encouraged more people to read newspapers, which included coverage of local, national and international events. Consequently, the number of newspapers published in Ireland increased from seventy-three in 1849 to 122 in 1879.[33] Another important factor which made newspapers more accessible was that they became much more affordable as the nineteenth century progressed. During the 1850s the tax on advertisements was repealed, the compulsory stamp on newspapers was abolished and owing to techno-logical advances printing costs were reduced.[34] The price of the *Nation*, for instance decreased from 6*d.* in the 1840s to 2*d.* in 1868.[35] After 1880, there was an increasing demand for newspapers with a nationalist outlook, and in Westmeath this need was met in September 1882 by the founding of the *Westmeath Examiner*. The editorial states without reservation the main aim of the new newspaper:

> With regard to our objects, one of the principal aims of the *Examiner* will be to keep alive and intensify the spirit of self reliance which now pervades the people, to give greater facilities on all occasions for the free expression of the people's wishes, to so consolidate the popular opinions that they may be of most support to the Irish party, led by Mr Parnell.[36]

The spirit of this editorial obviously reflects the readership for which it was intended. It is worth noting that the paper was founded in response to a demand from a large group of people who believed that their views were not represented by the existing county newspaper, the conservative, pro-establish-ment *Westmeath Guardian*. This demand for a new newspaper, a direct outcome of increased literacy resulting from the expansion of primary education in the parish, was a major step forward in the process of modernisation. As Donnelly remarked on this point: 'Both the home rule and land movements depended upon mass support from a literate, avid newspaper reading public'.[37]

Given the wider world which the tenant farmers were interacting with in the post-Famine era, what was the level of their political awareness and involvement? Between the Famine and the land war, there arose many situations which would have stimulated political discussion amongst the tenant community in Collinstown. In 1850 the Tenant Right League in Westmeath highlighted many weaknesses in the tenant-landlord relations in the county. Rev. Michael Coghlan, the parish priest of Collinstown attended the inaugural meeting of the league in Mullingar and proposed the following resolution:

> That considering the prices of agricultural produce the time has come when an immediate and considerable reduction of rents is absolutely necessary to save the farmer from ruin – to enable him to employ the labourer and to discharge his just obligation to the landlord.[38]

For him it was imperative that a law should be passed to protect the tenants' interests in the face of unfair treatment at the hands of landlords. He favoured the constitutional method employed by the league in seeking their demands rather than by 'secret combination'. However, he acknowledged that there

were some 'noble-hearted and generous landlords' such as William Barlow
Smythe, a local resident landlord in Collinstown. He provided the following
glowing account of Smythe:

> Instead of evicting those who were unable to pay former high rents he
> has set them the example of working on their own farms, and allowed
> them liberally for fencing, draining, and subsoiling – independent of an
> ample allowance for the failure of the potato crop.

Overall, Coghlan was harsh in his criticism of the landlord community and
noted the fact that Smythe was 'an exception to his class'.[39] This relationship
was to sour somewhat two years later when a controversy arose between the
two men regarding the 1852 general election.[40] The Westmeath Farmers' Club,
in the early 1860s likewise generated considerable debate. Although this club
was geared towards the larger farmers, they had issues in common with smaller
tenants such as reforms of the land system and greater security of tenure.[41]
This vibrant group of farmers acted as a pressure group for parliamentary
reform on land issues: two of the four bills which were before the house of
commons in 1860 'to amend the law of landlord and tenant' were prepared
and submitted by the Westmeath Farmers' Club.[42] They held several public
meetings and their activities were widely reported in the *Westmeath Guardian*.[43]

General elections also generated political discussion and these provided the
battlefield for the ideological war which was waged between the landlord
community and the Catholic clergy. The clash between Smythe and the Catholic
clergy in Collinstown in the 1852 general election provides an example of this
conflict in the parish of Collinstown and will be treated in greater detail in the
following section. However, in spite of the stimulating political environment
in Westmeath, meaningful participation in politics was beyond the reach of the
vast majority of tenants. At the most basic level, this is reflected in the number
of people who were eligible to vote. In 1862, the Westmeath electorate was
approximately 3,653, which was 14.6 per cent of the adult male population.[44]
In 1871, only one in six adult males was entitled to vote in Ireland, as opposed
to one in three in England and Scotland in 1869.[45] Granted, occupiers of all
holdings valued above £4, as well as all landowners were entitled to vote in
the annual poor law elections, and there were tenant representatives in the
elected half of these bodies, the other half being appointed. However, prior to
the land war, the offices of the poor law boards were dominated by landowners.
In 1877, for instance, 87 per cent of the offices at national level were held by
landowners.[46] What alternative route was open to tenants who wished to
become politically active? Comerford underlines the point that most people
attracted to the fenian movement did not have direct access to parliamentary
politics.[47] This undoubtedly was an influential factor in the growth of
fenianism in Westmeath before the 1867 rising. The railway also played a role

in this growth. As in other counties, railway employees were particularly targeted as these were perceived as being strategically valuable in the event of a rising and consequently, railway workers were recruited in Mullingar and Multyfarnham. There was also evidence of fenianism in other parts of the county, among them Castlepollard, Delvin and Finea, all in north Westmeath.[48] In the decade after the rising, fenian membership experienced a significant increase in Westmeath. The publicity generated by the Amnesty Movement undoubtedly had an influence, and indeed Mullingar was selected to be one of the locations of the 'amnesty meetings' which took place between July and October 1869. The Amnesty Association, chaired by Isaac Butt, campaigned for the release of fenian prisoners serving sentences in British prisons. A crowd of 10,000 is reputed to have attended in Mullingar on 29 August 1869, supervised by some 1,000 members of the R.I.C.[49] Estimates of fenian membership for Westmeath indicate that approximately 256 people were members in 1868. By 1878 this had increased to 500.[50] There is evidence which indicates that the fenian movement gained a foothold in the parish of Collinstown. Patrick Cole stated in his evidence at the Barbavilla trials that in 1867 he had joined the Fenian Brotherhood, but that after his marriage in 1873 he had stopped attending meetings.[51] Peter Fagan, a labourer from Benison Lodge (a townland also known as Bratty) was listed in police files as belonging to the fenian society in Westmeath in August 1882.[52] Pat Fitzsimons and Michael Fagan, were both in their twenties and belonged to the new generation of fenians. The former was a carpenter from Glenidan and worked locally.[53] Fagan worked as a blacksmith in Dublin since June 1880, and became heavily involved in the fenian movement, becoming a 'centre' for the organisation in the city.[54] He was later to be executed for his part in the atrocity known as the 'Phoenix Park Murders', when a group calling themselves the 'National Invincibles', murdered the chief secretary, Lord Frederick Cavendish, and the under-secretary, T.H. Burke, whilst they were walking in the Phoenix Park shortly after Cavendish's arrival in Dublin, on 6 May 1882.

In spite of the stimulus provided for political life in the county by organisations such as the Tenant Right League and the Westmeath Farmers' Club, there were very limited opportunities for participation in politics for the majority of tenants and for some, fenianism presented itself as an alternative means of belonging to a political group. Nevertheless, the growth in political awareness among the tenants in Westmeath, and indeed throughout Ireland, was a development which was a significant factor in mobilising tenants to become involved in the Land League agitation of the late 1870s and early 1880s.

The Land War, 1879–82

Following a period of general economic improvement, tenant farmers were faced with a serious depression in the late 1870s which affected all sectors of the farming community, especially those engaged in tillage. Adverse weather conditions, poor harvests and falling prices all contributed to the hardship which resulted from this depression. Such was the level of distress by 1879, that the Conservative administration appointed a commission to investigate the depressed condition of Irish agriculture. William Evans of Gilliardstown House, which is located in the parish of Collinstown, gave evidence before this commission in November 1880. When asked whether the farmers in his area had been badly affected by the recent agricultural depression he replied that:

> As a body I should say they have been affected very much by recent circumstances. First of all by the depression in trade, next by being brought into close contact with America, and thirdly (which in my mind affected them more than anything else) by the bad season that we have had.[1]

The year 1879 was the wettest year on record. According to the observations on the produce of crops in the agricultural statistics for the Delvin area, the cold wet summer had a devastating affect on the potato crop, which in many cases was 'more than half diseased'.[2] Figure 1 illustrates the effect on the

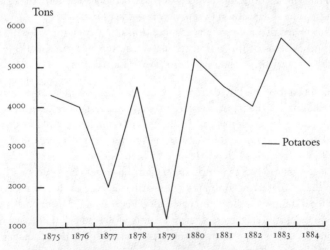

1. Estimated produce of potatoes Delvin Poor Law Union, *1875–85*

produce of potatoes that year. The pig population, which was dependent on the potato crop for food, was consequently affected. In fact, the number of pigs in Westmeath plummeted in 1880 to the level they were at in 1848, which was the lowest on record.[3]

The abnormally high rainfall not only affected crops, as it stimulated grass growth, which in turn encouraged the spread of disease among livestock.[4] According to an observation made by a member of the Royal Irish Constabulary in the Mullingar area, the yield of hay 'would have been much larger had the summer been warmer; a great deal was lost when cut'.[5] The cattle population of the Delvin poor law union fell by 11 per cent between 1879 and 1880.[6] The situation was exacerbated by the fact that prices for store cattle fell in 1879 by 5 per cent and for 2–3 year-olds by 8 per cent from the average price in the period 1871–76.[7] Farmers bringing livestock to fairs throughout Ireland in the autumn of 1879 found it very difficult to find buyers. A reporter from the *Westmeath Guardian* attended the October fair in Killucan, ten miles from Collinstown, and commenting on the depressed prices he observed that: 'It is no wonder to find the tenantry in general appealing to the generosity of their landlords to tide them over this unpleasant season'.[8]

The depression made a noticeable impact on the number of people seeking poor law relief in the union of Delvin which increased by 33 per cent between June 1878 and June 1879.[9] Labourers were particularly hard hit as the economic decline affected farmers' ability to employ them. This, together with the failure of the potato crop would have undoubtedly swelled the numbers seeking relief. In September, a resolution passed at the meeting of the board of guardians for the Poor Law Union of Delvin was published in the *Westmeath Guardian*:

> That on account of a succession of bad harvests and the general agricultural depression that has set into the country, it is the opinion of this board that a considerable reduction of rents ought to be made by the landlords of this union to enable the tenant farmers to tide over these trying times and save them from national ruin.[10]

This had been proposed by Patrick Cole, one of the local fenians referred to earlier. Although his concern was undoubtedly sincere, as a shopkeeper he was very likely suffering from the impact of the depression himself as a result of the reduced purchasing power of his customers. During the prosperous years of the 1870s, shopkeepers had extended credit to their customers, but with the hard times of the depression they no longer had the resources to do this.[11] This affected the whole tenant community, but particularly the small farmers, as these had to depend more on shop-purchased food because of the poor potato yield.

To what degree did the crisis affect tenants' ability to pay their rent? Since the rental for this period is not extant in the Smythe of Barbavilla papers, the rental of the Smyth estate in nearby Drumcree was examined in order to

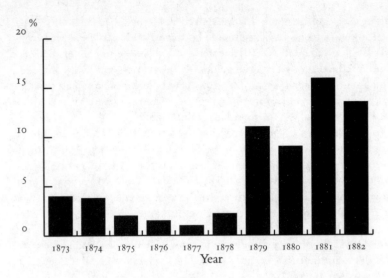

2. Arrears as percentage of annual rent, Drumcree estate, 1873–1882.

evaluate the impact of the agricultural depression in terms of the number of tenants who fell into arrears.[12]

Figure 2 illustrates the percentage of rent due which was in arrears over a nine-year period and indicates, as might be expected, that there was a significant increase during the period 1879–82. In 1881 16 per cent of the rent due was in arrears on the Drumcree estate. Vaughan has analysed arrears as a percentage of rent due in twelve different estates throughout Ireland. For the year 1881, eleven estates had surviving records, and six of these had arrears which were higher than 16 per cent of the rent due, the highest being 57 per cent (two estates).[13] His findings demonstrate that there were estates where the agricultural depression had a far more serious impact on the tenants' ability to pay the rent. In the case of the Drumcree estate the recovery in the yield of potatoes in 1880 (see figure 1) may have averted a more serious crisis.

When it came to paying rent during an agricultural depression some landlords voluntarily, or in response to a request from their tenants, granted an abatement in the rent. William Barlow Smythe reminded his tenants in October 1881 that he was the first landlord to 'voluntarily and publicly' grant a 10 per cent reduction on the May rents of 1879, if the rent were paid by November.[14] He also admitted that he had allowed an abatement in the May rents of 1881 'not for justice but for peace sake'.[15] On 10 October 1881, the *Westmeath Guardian* announced that the agents for the Smyths of Drumcree were granting the tenants a 20 per cent reduction on rents. It was also pointed out that there had been no increases in rent on this estate over the previous twenty years.[16] Other local landlords who publicly announced abatements during 1881 included Sir Richard Levinge, Knockdrin Castle (10 to 25 per cent in 1881) and Charles B. Marley, Belvedere House (20 per cent in 1880).[17] Such announcements however, should be viewed with a cold eye as in many cases landlords granted 'selective abatements', therefore not all tenants were granted reductions by this arrangement.[18] In addition, as Clark concludes, reductions of this kind were quite inadequate in terms of providing relief for the tenant. Of course, in some instances no abatements were given and this had a major bearing on the founding of the Land League.

In the autumn of 1879 the tenants in the west of Ireland found themselves in dire circumstances as a result of the agricultural depression. Mass demonstrations were organised to demand rent reductions and to protest against evictions. Local agitation was initiated in Irishtown, County Mayo, by a group of Mayo fenians in April 1879. The success of this event precipitated further agitation and by 21 October 1879 the need for a national organisation was responded to by the founding of the Irish National Land League, with Charles Stewart Parnell as president.[19] In the immediate term its main goal was the reduction of rents. Griffith's valuation (1848–60) was deemed by the league to be the appropriate level at which to pay. The long-term objective of the league was in theory to secure peasant proprietorship. Although this was clearly part of the Land League programme and often featured in resolutions passed at demonstration meetings, Clark argues that the emphasis that peasant proprietorship received should not be exaggerated.[20] In a sample of resolutions, he found that those calling for a reduction in rent or a halt to evictions were more numerous than resolutions advocating peasant proprietorship.[21] Interestingly, peasant proprietorship featured in all of the Land League meetings held in Westmeath which were reported in the *Westmeath Guardian* in the winter of 1880. This can be accounted for by the fact that the two Westmeath M.P.s, T.D. Sullivan and G.H. Gill, were involved in these meetings and nationalist politicians emphasised peasant proprietorship in the belief that it furthered the nationalist cause.[22] Many features of the customary agrarian code were incorporated into Land League propaganda, such as the famous phrase 'Keep a firm grip on your homesteads'.[23] Parnell's recommendation regarding tenants who had taken a holding from which others had been evicted also reflected a traditional method which had long been employed in rural Ireland, that is the placing of such tenants in a 'moral Coventry'. As Townshend has argued, 'the Land League, in its local manifestation, was in many ways just the biggest and most successful of the old associations'.[24]

In all, County Westmeath hosted sixteen Land League demonstration meetings, the highest number in Leinster during the years 1879 and 1880.[25] Fourteen of the sixteen meetings took place after 1 October 1880. It would seem that from November 1880, the movement began to gather momentum, and newspaper coverage indicates that the local leadership for this body in County Westmeath was provided by the two local M.P.s, Sullivan and Gill. The latter had been a town commissioner in Dublin corporation prior to his election to parliament in 1880.[26] Sullivan's impeccable nationalist credentials included the editorship of the nationalist paper the *Nation*, which he had taken over from his brother A.M. Sullivan in 1876, and membership of the central committee of the Land League. In addition, he was the composer of the ballad 'God save Ireland' in 1867, which became the anthem of nationalism in Ireland in the late-nineteenth century. The leadership of the league in Westmeath by two members of parliament was typical of the Land League in Leinster, where in contrast with Connacht, constitutionalists rather than fenians provided the driving force.[27]

The Collinstown and Fore branch of the League was founded in November 1880.[28] The chairman was the local Roman Catholic curate, Rev. Patrick O'Reilly. William Mc Cormack from Ballinavine was treasurer and Francis Adlum from Clondalever was the secretary.[29] These two men were substantial farmers: McCormack was a grazier with a holding of approximately 400 statute acres, while Adlum's was approximately 200 statute acres.[30] 'C. Flynn' was the under-secretary, and is likely to have come from Glenidan as four Flynns are listed in Griffith's valuation for that townland, all of them holding less than twenty acres.[31] William Woods from Collinstown was referred to later on as 'member of the council', but his particular office was not specified. The inclusion among the officers of 'strong farmers' from the tenant community, Mc Cormack and Adlum, was typical of the Land League leadership.[32] This can also be said of the position of chairman held by the local Catholic curate. The local Catholic bishop, William Nulty, supported the Land League and was among the speakers who addressed the demonstration meeting in Mullingar.[33] Judging by the long lists of priests who attended demonstration meetings, the Catholic clergy in County Westmeath actively supported the movement. At the same time, unlike earlier movements in the nineteenth century such as the repeal movement, in this case they followed rather than led the Land League.[34]

Members of the Collinstown and Fore branch of the Land League had access to many large demonstration meetings within reach of the parish. One such demonstration which had been organised by the Delvin and Killucan branches took place at Killough on 1 November 1880.[35] Other demonstration meetings took place in Finea and Mountnugent on 7 November 1880, Clonmellon on the 12 December, and Mullingar on 19 December, at which the crowd was believed to be in excess of 10,000.[36] In the new year, a meeting took place in Castlepollard, three miles from Collinstown, which was reported to have attracted a crowd of 12,000.[37] Given that this estimated number of people in attendance was being reported in the pro-nationalist press it is likely that it was somewhat exaggerated. According to newspaper reports, people came from Longford and Cavan to attend this gathering, and 'large and well ordered bodies' from various parts of Westmeath were listed including one from Collinstown. The purpose of these meetings was to clearly state the demands of the Land League and encourage local support for the movement. In some instances, such as an earlier meeting in the spring of 1880 which took place in the neighbouring parish of Mountnugent, County Cavan, mass demonstrations were organised to express 'indignation' at a threatened eviction. In this case, a local agent, Matthew Weld O'Connor, had served ejectments on a number of tenants. These were not named in the newspaper report, but were more than likely the seven tenants in the Kilbride area who were evicted two months later.[38] Other unacceptable practices of Weld O'Connor's were highlighted such as charging rents 50–60 per cent above Griffith's valuation and not allowing any reductions in rents during the late agricultural depression. Joseph Biggar, M.P. for Cavan, addressed the meeting and according to the newspaper report advocated the boycott of the Weld O'Connor family.[39] This meeting pre-dated the famous Captain Boycott affair which occurred the following October and November, therefore the term 'boycott' was not used.

The pageantry attached to these outings added colour and drama to the Land League movement. In Castlepollard, a flavour of the heady atmosphere is captured by the description in the newspaper report of the 'tastefully decorated' arches bearing such mottoes as 'Parnell is our Leader' and 'God save Ireland'. Flags with the national emblem inscribed on them were specially prepared for the day and were apparently floating out of every window.[40] Music also played a significant part in setting the mood, and at the Mullingar meeting, bands 'paraded the streets during the day playing a variety of national airs'.[41] Tenants were drawn to these occasions, not alone on account of the cause they supported, but because they were colourful, exciting social events. The railway had an important role to play in the proceedings. Not only could it whisk Sullivan or Gill down from Dublin to attend the meetings and allow them to return the same day, but it also played a part in the ritual of their arrival. A deputation of the most prominent Land League members in the area greeted the politicians at the railway station, and from there they were brought in a 'brake' to the venue for the meeting, or for some pre-meeting refreshments.[42] For some meetings, such as the Mullingar meeting, the Midland Railway Company laid on extra trains to accommodate the large crowds expected to attend. All the newspaper reports emphasised the peaceful and orderly nature of these meetings. However this belied the situation in the county regarding agrarian crime. According to parliamentary returns, agrarian crime significantly increased in County Westmeath during the land war: thirty-six agrarian crimes were recorded for 1879, thirty-five for 1880.[43] This shot up to 100 for the following year.[44] In the combined total of agrarian crimes reported during these three years, Westmeath was the second most disturbed county in Leinster, the first being King's County which saw an increase of agrarian crime from 39 in 1879 to 154 in 1881.[45] Kilkenny, which held third place also experienced a dramatic increase from eight to 113. By 27 December 1881 Westmeath was declared a 'proclaimed district', requiring an additional establishment of police.[46]

As in the tradition of the old associations, violence helped to enforce the 'laws' of the Land League. Although Land League leaders repeatedly condemned violence in public, the agitation associated with the league in some instances created an atmosphere which encouraged disorder.[47] This is well illustrated at the

Mullingar meeting, where Thomas Brennan, secretary of the Land League, addressed the crowd. While he joined with his colleagues in condemning violence, 'he at the same time knew that human nature is human nature, and that as long as outrages are practised on the people there will always be reprisals'. He added that the threatened suspension of the *habeas corpus* was an attack on the people of Ireland outside the constitution and that 'the people would feel they had a right to defend themselves outside the constitution'.[48] Brennan, an ex-fenian leader, was known to be one of the more radical members of the executive council of the Land League.[49] Speeches such as this practically endorsed the use of violence and clearly justified its use. Such authorisations by the secretary of the National Land League, no doubt gave this sanction extra weight in the ears of some of the listeners.

During the meeting in Mullingar at which Brennan spoke, Robert Nolan, a tenant farmer from the Killucan branch of the Land League, proposed the following: 'we also enter our strongest protest against the eleven month's grass farm system, which in this particular county has worked such bitter ruin'.[50] Similarly, a resolution passed by the Collinstown and Fore branch of the Land League and published in the *Nation* in April 1881 also expressed anti-grazier sentiments:

> That we condemn in the most emphatic manner the conduct of those
> who in the neighbouring districts are taking grasslands from landlords
> at high rents, under the nine or ten months' system contrary to the vital
> principle of the league'.[51]

This would strongly suggest that the tensions which characterised the 1869–71 period of unrest were still evident. These grievances no doubt acted as an effective motivating factor in mobilising local tenant farmers to become involved in the league. It is interesting to note that this resolution was proposed, given that graziers such as McCormack were involved in the leadership of the branch. Involvement at officer level meant that large farmers could protect their own interests and consequently exercise some measure of control over resolutions.[52] Therefore different people joined the Land League for different and often diametrically opposed reasons. It must be emphasised however, that there is no documentary evidence to establish conclusively that either McCormack, or indeed, Adlum, held land under the eleven-month system, but clearly the possibility should not be ruled out. The broad appeal the Land League held for tenants across the spectrum of landholding sizes played an important role in attracting tenants into its ranks. The majority of resolutions which were passed at branch and demonstration meetings were based on interests which were relevant to the needs of large and small farmers.[53] An example of such a resolution was passed at a meeting in September 1881 by the Collinstown and Fore branch: 'We heartily congratulate the tenants of Gilliardstown on their determined stand in their defence of their first rights, and in opposition to landlord tyranny'. In this instance they were opposing the 'cruel and tyrannical' action of a local landlord

Ellis, who refused to allow an abatement in the rent.[54] Gilliardstown was a townland of mixed farm sizes. Opposition to adverse landlord activity was an area in which large and small tenants alike shared a common objective.

From June 1880 onwards, Land League leaders advocated a policy whereby tenants were advised to delay in paying unjust rents for as long as possible and only to do so as a last resort. The Land League met the expenses incurred by the tenant as a result of the delay. This inconvenienced landlords and deprived them of the interest on the rent.[55] In many of the earlier instances landlords in straitened circumstances were prepared to accept a reduced rent.[56] However, once it became known that the tenants would eventually pay the rent and that the Land League would pay the legal costs of the delay, many landlords held out for the full rent.[57] It was a costly and impractical policy but nevertheless the Land League persevered with it well into 1881. In Collinstown parish, a tenant in Gilliardstown held out 'to the point of a bayonet' in April 1881. This was Patrick McCormack, who was served a writ in the spring of 1881 as he had refused to pay the year's rent he owed, which was £185. At a meeting of the Collinstown and Fore branch of the Land League which took place on 11 April 1881, a resolution was passed thanking McCormack for 'his conduct in this matter'.[58] The following July he had to bid for his farm at the sheriff's sale in Mullingar and the branch applied to the central committee for reimbursement of legal costs which came to £18. 10s. 0d. and were duly forwarded on 9 July.[59] It would seem that by refusing to pay this large rent until at the 'point of a bayonet', the local branch of the league highlighted the injustice they attributed to the inflexibility of Ellis, the landlord in question.

Although women became members of the Land League, the dictates of social conventions at the time restricted the extent to which they could become actively involved. A development in 1880 changed this situation and allowed for fuller participation of women in Land League activity. In the autumn of 1880, Parnell's sister Fanny, then living in the United States, was dismayed to learn that financial contributions to the Land League had decreased, and was concerned about the effect this would have on the agitation.[60] She responded with an alternative idea for fund-raising: groups of women could come together and form a Ladies' Land League, charging a dollar for membership, and initiate fund-raising events, the proceeds of which were to be forwarded to the Land League. Accordingly, the Ladies' Land League was founded in New York on 12 October 1880, with Parnell's mother Delia as president. It was a successful venture and in January 1881, with the prospect of many of the Land League leaders being jailed, Davitt proposed that a similar body should be founded in Ireland with Anna Parnell at its head. It was to be responsible for relieving distress among evicted families, and support for the families of men who would be imprisoned as a result of the Coercion Act, which was soon to be passed.[61] The second purpose was, in Davitt's words, 'to keep up a semblance of organisation during the attempted repression I saw coming'.[62] Thus the Ladies' Land League was formed on 31 January 1881, and branches were soon founded all over Ireland.

A branch was promptly founded in Mullingar, as an address to Anna Parnell was published in the *Westmeath Guardian* in February 1881. This was presented to her in the ladies' cloakroom of the train station in Mullingar, at which Parnell had to stop briefly on her journey to Carrick-on-Shannon. The venue is noteworthy, as women were unaccustomed to speaking publicly, as indeed was the public to listening to female orators. Perhaps the crowded platform on which men and women thronged to greet Parnell was perceived to be an inappropriate place to deliver an address by the women themselves, given the social mores of the time. The whole issue of women speaking in public was particularly offensive to some Catholic bishops, such as Archbishop Edward Mc Cabe of Dublin, who instructed the men in his flock not to 'tolerate the woman who so far disavows her birthright of modesty as to parade herself before the public gaze . . .'.[63] In some instances the Catholic clergy defended the Ladies' Land League, but usually this was on the basis that it was a charitable organisation and therefore an acceptable extension of women's role as wife and mother.[64] This was the view of the Ladies' Land League shared by the Rev. John Curry, parish priest of Collinstown in 1884. It was communicated in correspondence with the commissioners of education regarding a controversy which arose from the fact that subscriptions for the Ladies' Land League had been collected at Collinstown National School in the spring of 1881.[65]

The Fore Branch of the Ladies Land League was founded in February 1881. Among its officers were Margaret Gallagher, secretary and Anne Fitzsimons, treasurer.[66] Also active in the branch were Rebecca Mc Cormack and Mary Cantwell from Gilliardstown.[67] Both of these had relatives who were involved in the Land League, as indeed had Mary Tuite who presented the address in Mullingar.[68] This was a typical feature of women who were active in the Ladies' Land League, both at the central and local level. It could also be said that at both levels it attracted middle-class women, many of them young and single. All of the women of the Fore branch, whose names appeared in the *Nation*, were single.[69] This branch met weekly and occasionally the resolutions passed at their meetings were forwarded and published in the *Nation* or *United Ireland*. At a meeting on the 12 February 1882, a resolution was passed which called on the government to 'release Mr Parnell and others suspects'.[70] On 2 April 1882, the day of the Barbavilla murder, the branch organised a bazaar in the grounds of the church in Fore and raised £39. 4s. 0d. which was forwarded to the central committee.[71] The Prevention of Crime (Ireland) Act, passed by the government in order to bring perpetrators of serious outrages within the reach of the law, was met with strong disapproval in July:[72]

> We, the members of this branch at the first meeting after the crime bill became law, most emphatically protest against a measure passed by a so-

called representative assembly of legislators, when in fact the representatives
of the people for whom the act is intended were silenced and expelled from
the house of commons during the most important part of said act . . .[73]

The various resolutions which were published indicate that politics was a
much-discussed topic at these meetings. Providing relief and assistance for
tenants families and prisoners was an important function of the Fore branch.
In a letter to the central committee they expressed their thanks for the £5
which they had received for the family of a man who was in prison, referred
to as 'Fagan, the suspect'.[74] In Collinstown the branch provided shelter for an
evicted family in the spring of 1882. In May 1882, Gallagher visited Mary O'
Connor – sister of T.P. O' Connor – who was in prison in Mullingar, and
reported that 'she was in good health and no way discouraged by her recent
imprisonment'.[75] Although these activities highlight the relief aspect of the
organisation, they undoubtedly carry a political message as well. Effectively the
women were making a statement by these actions; on the one hand they were
relieving distress, on the other hand they were challenging what was seen to
be the source of that distress, which was landlordism.

When Charles Stewart Parnell and a number of prominent Land League
leaders were arrested in October 1881, they issued a manifesto from Kilmainham
jail which became known as the 'no rent manifesto'.[76] This directed tenants to
pay 'no rents under any circumstances until the government relinquishes the
existing system of terrorism and restores the constitutional rights of the
people'.[77] This new development was aimed at appeasing the more militant
element of the league, particularly in the United States where the league
received important financial backing. It would seem that the signatories did
not expect it to receive strong backing from the league and indeed the
response to this directive was mixed. Obviously the more radical members of
the league welcomed it, but it was received with little or no enthusiasm by the
moderate element and with hostility by the majority of Catholic bishops, even
including passionate Land League supporters such as Bishop Thomas Croke.
The challenge of the manifesto was taken up by some tenants in Collinstown
which suggests there were some extreme elements in the local Land League.
Later at the Barbavilla trials, the mother of one of the prisoners related in her
evidence that during the manifesto she had two farms and refused to pay the
rent on one of them owing to 'all the outrages going on in the country'.[78]
John McGrath, one of the prisoners had paid his rent on the Barbavilla estate
throughout the 'no rent manifesto' and was unpopular as a result.[79]
Understandably the 'no rent manifesto' antagonised Smythe and placed the
increasingly fragile relationship with his tenants under further strain.

Smythe had been eulogised locally in 1868, when 'Kennedy', a labourer in
Collinstown, wrote the following verse:

> Come all you noble Irishmen that live in Erin's land,
> I hope you'll pay attention and this to understand,
> I mean to sound my praise with all my noted skill,
> Concerning the great gentleman that lives in Barbaville.[80]

'The great gentleman' inherited Barbavilla when he came of age in 1830. He had been awarded a double first class degree at Christ Church, Oxford, and afterwards a M.A. degree from Trinity College, Dublin. He resided on the estate and was active in local government, serving on the board of the poor law guardians in Delvin, the lunatic asylum in Mullingar, and as justice of the peace in Collinstown. The estate in Westmeath consisted of 2,108 acres.[81] He remained master of Barbavilla for over fifty years.

During his time as landlord, he made various improvements on the estate such as the award-winning cottages built in the village of Collinstown in 1860. On the face of it, he would seem to have been on good terms with most of his tenants. In a letter sent to them shortly before the murder he addresses them as 'friends'.[82] Moreover, he did not have a reputation for evicting tenants: Richard Riggs, whom he evicted in 1882, was the first tenant he had ever evicted on account of non-payment of rent. Even a threatening letter sent in 1880 to the agent for the Barbavilla estate acknowledged that Smythe was a good employer.[83] After the murder, Smythe's reputation for being a good landlord was highlighted by the outraged *Westmeath Guardian* who described him as 'one of the most generous landowners in Westmeath' and that his life had been one of 'beneficence, of charity, and of good works'.[84] Why should such a landlord be the target for assassination? An important consideration revealed by the various sources was Smythe's strong propensity for 'going public' with his personal views, particularly about politics and religion. His chief *modus operandi* was to write letters to the newspapers, but when a local controversy arose in which he felt compelled to outline in a forthright manner his views on a matter, he sometimes published notices for local distribution. The reason why he chose to do this is not entirely clear, but it was more than likely to ensure that his message would be guaranteed to reach the people for whom it was intended.

A series of Smythe's letters to the newspapers were featured in the summer of 1852, when a war of words was waged in the pages of the *Westmeath Guardian* between Smythe and the two Catholic clerics of Collinstown.[85] Both the landlord and the priests felt entitled to direct the local tenants as to whom they should vote for in the general election of August 1852. The landlord's candidate won, but the battle apparently was not over, as Smythe wrote to Rev. Coghlan that he had been informed

> ... that there is an intention on the part of some of your flock, sooner or later, to gratify their fiendish and avowed malice against all who voted for Sir Richard Levinge about here, and against all Protestants. Now, sir, I announce plainly that, whatever may be my present resolves, I shall feel it

my duty to remove one Roman Catholic tenant for every such outrage, whoever may be the guilty party; and further, that in case of what is called 'popular vengeance' falling upon myself for so doing, I have taken measures to secure that a just civil retribution shall fall upon this estate, such as would make many a one deplore for the rest of their lives that any listened to such fatal suggestions.[86]

Fortunately, no outrage occurred to necessitate this course of action but it undoubtedly had a damaging effect on the relationship between Smythe and his Catholic tenantry. The rights and duties of an owner of property, and his discomfort with Catholics were two recurring themes of Smythe's communications. The following decade, Smythe was invited in January 1863 by a group of people – mainly Roman Catholic clergy and tenant farmers in Westmeath – to discuss the Tenant Right Bill. He declined and outlined his reasons for doing so in a letter, a copy of which he forwarded for publication to the *Westmeath Guardian*. In Smythe's opinion, the depressed condition of the Irish people was not 'in consequence of the injustice of existing relations between landlord and tenant'. The root of the discontent lay elsewhere:

> I believe the condition of the Irish people would be very different from what it is were they not instructed in discontent from the cradle, and taught to regard everyone in at all a better position – especially if of another denomination in religion – as their natural antagonist or enemy.[87]

This effectively demonstrates the weakness of the social bond between Smythe and the tenant community, in spite of his many positive characteristics as a landlord. Smythe's anti-Catholicism, evident here as it was in the 1852 election controversy, was a phenomenon which was prevalent in Victorian England, where Smythe was educated. He particularly regarded the Catholic clergy with antipathy and distrust. This is not surprising given the fact that the Catholic clergy played an active role in the challenge to the largely Protestant landlord community. The insecurity which is evident in the above passage was to increase during the land war. Smythe found himself caught between the Liberal party on one hand, as they instigated increased intervention between landlord and tenant in the passing of the 1881 Land Act, and the tenants on the other hand who were collectively agitating for change.[88] For Smythe this had the effect of seriously undermining the rights of property owners. For instance, he believed the extension of the 'Ulster custom' to the other three provinces to be 'a present to the tenants to the detriment of the landlords' and that it was 'wrong in principle'.[89] The combination of Land League activity in Ireland and political developments in Westminster where the Liberals were in power would appear to have influenced the stance which Smythe was later to adopt in relation to the Riggs case. The events at Barbavilla on 2 April 1882 brought all these issues sharply into focus and ensured that Smythe's public profile extended far beyond County Westmeath.

'Another Shocking Murder in Westmeath'[1]

The Riggs family had been tenants on the Barbavilla estate for three generations at least, as Smythe made reference to Riggs's father and grandfather in *The Tale of Westmeath, Wickedness and Woe* (1882). Their holding, a farm of sixty-seven statute acres was valued at £68. 10s. 0d. in 1854 according to Griffith's valuation and the rent for the property was £76.[2] Shortly after the murder, Smythe referring to Richard Riggs in a letter to E. Brice states that:

> the evicted man or _____? [sic] had been getting worse and worse for 16 or 18 years, an utter beggar from his own conduct with a moderate rent, no stock, always in arrears only paying for the past by bills of men to whom he was allowed to sub-let for the future . . .[3]

In the opening paragraph of his pamphlet, Smythe refers to Riggs's financial difficulties, stating that it was not for him 'to say *how* they arose'.[4] The available documentary evidence is equally opaque on this point. However, local oral testimony suggests that Riggs had a strong partiality for alcoholic drink.[5] One account describes how he tied the horses to the handle of the plough one morning, intending to plough a field, but ended up in the village of Collinstown where he spent the remainder of the day drinking. The following morning the horses and plough which had been left unattended since the previous morning were observed by people on their way to Mass.[6] This fondness for drink may have been responsible for Riggs's 'hopeless insolvency' which Smythe referred to in a communication with Dublin Castle, after the murder.[7]

In the *Tale of Wesmeath*, Smythe also refers to the fact that the rent for the Riggs holding was paid only in arrears for at least seventeen years.[8] Accordingly, Smythe allowed Riggs to sub-let meadow, grass and conacre from time to time in anticipation that such arrangements would generate sufficient income for him to pay his debts. In 1879, according to Smythe, this system collapsed: Riggs could not 'raise any money having neither stock nor credit . . . he could pay no rent and his land was becoming impoverished . . .'.[9] The ejectment *habere* was taken out in January 1880 and executed in March of the same year.[10] Riggs accused Smythe of evicting him because he had converted to Roman Catholicism some twenty years earlier, an accusation which the latter strongly denied, and he pointed to another case of a Catholic tenant in difficulty on the estate which was being amicably settled.[11] It seems likely, given Smythe's rigid views on Catholicism, that Riggs's conversion would not have been regarded favourably by Smythe. However, he had been permitted to remain on the estate for approximately twenty years in spite of his financial difficulties and therefore it would seem on balance that his religious affiliation in this instance was not the issue.[12] The available evidence would suggest that Smythe was reacting against the Land League agitation, and in the climate which prevailed at this time, felt compelled to assert his rights as a landowner.

After the general election of March 1880 which saw the Liberals back in power, parliamentary politics also coloured Smythe's perception of the situation landlords were facing in Ireland. As an avid supporter of the Conservative party, he viewed Liberal policy in Ireland with a jaundiced eye, in particular its tolerance of the Land League, as he saw it, and its reluctance to implement more stringent laws in the face of growing disorder. This was evident in a letter written to the chief secretary, W.E. Forster, on 3 December 1880 when he informed him that:

> . . . there is to be an important Land League meeting near here on Sunday, the 12th when the teachings, which the *doctrinaires* of your cabinet took no step to discountenance for months, and even now have taken no step to suppress, will, doubtless, be poured into ears, which have not yet heard them – teachings which you have allowed to sink so deep among many, that it will take a generation, under a better moral policy, to unteach.[13]

In March 1880, Smythe made Riggs an offer of 'forgiveness of £152, and £70 to go away', which he refused and was reinstated in the house as caretaker, in order to give him a final opportunity to pay his rent and arrears in six months.[14] However, Riggs's situation did not improve and during the month of October 1880, shortly before his case was due to come up again before the petty sessions, Anthony Sutton, the agent at Barbavilla received a threatening letter. Riggs's case was receiving attention from the unofficial upholders of the traditional code.

Committee Rooms

> Sir, – It has come under our notice, this tyrannical and oppressive act which is about to be executed on the property of Barbavilla; and for the third and last time our committee has come to the conclusion what to do. We have made a careful inquiry into the case, and had not for a friend of yours, you were now cold in the clay. But it was stated that you were a charitable man some time ago, and your landlord a good employer. Had not for that you would not get this chance; but if you proceed with this case of eviction, come weal, come woe – we will proceed also at the risk of our lives, and when you and your landlord will least expect it. –
> Signed at headquarters,
>
> RORY OF THE HILLS.
>
> P.S. – If words won't do, active action must be.[15]

This was followed a few days later by another letter which included the following: 'I suppose you want the land for yourself or for some friend. *Dear land, bought by blood*. No Land League, none required; Lord Mountmorres fell; so will Minor Smyth and his tyrannical gent . . .'.[16] Smythe had these two letters published subsequently in the *Westmeath Guardian* in October 1880. Following the letters he included his own account of the facts, and concluded that the only crime he committed was 'of being born a landlord'.[17] One wonders at Smythe's lack of caution in drawing attention to the case in this way, in view of the fact that Land League agitation was gathering momentum in Westmeath at this time. The letter exuded an aura of confidence in the course of action he had adopted with Riggs. From Smythe's point of view the facts, as outlined in his account of his dealings with Riggs, should justify the eviction. Furthermore, by publishing the threatening letters, Smythe demonstrated that he had further grounds to proceed with the eviction, especially if he succeeded in linking the threatening letters with Riggs. He wrote: '. . . if he [Riggs] is found to be connected with the proposal *to pay in lead*, or that anything of that kind occur, he and his family shall forthwith be removed from the house which is no longer his'.[18]

In mid-November, Riggs broke the locks to the farm, and installed a number of cattle on the property, an action which provoked Smythe to proceed against him for trespass. The case came up at the petty sessions in Collinstown on 20 November 1880 and on this occasion, Smythe addressed a crowded court outlining his stance *vis-à-vis* Riggs. Before he left the bench, he seized the opportunity to give a discourse on the general state of the country. He wrote an account of it the following day in a letter to the chief secretary, W.E. Forster:

> I then deprecated the terrible agitation in the country, fomented by a Biggar, who had publicly expressed his hope, at a dinner given to Mr Parnell, of a more successful Hartmann at home! and by a Redpath, who had inculcated contempt and hatred in all a little better than themselves; I reminded them that 'whoso hateth his brother was a murderer' – that we saw the fruit of the agitation approaching us rapidly in the shooting of Colonel Cooper's steward near Mullingar.[19]

After making the above speech in a market house which was packed with supporters of the very people he was denouncing, Smythe wrote afterwards that he was 'listened to with attention, and, I was told, with some approval'.[20] As in the case of the threatening letters, deliberately attracting publicity would appear to be a highly imprudent course of action to adopt, given the political climate of the times. For whom the speech was ultimately intended best explains Smythe's behaviour at this point. Although delivered to an audience consisting mainly of tenant farmers in a small village in Westmeath, Smythe's sights were firmly placed on Forster, for whom he would write an account of the court case the following day. Quoting his speech and providing an account of the proceedings at the petty sessions afforded Smythe an ideal opportunity to criticise the Liberal administration in Ireland, as the following passage demonstrates:

> I have only in conclusion to tell you, that there is an organised disorganisation rapidly spreading over Ireland, which must soon, as it is intended, make it impossible for any government to rule Ireland except by martial law . . .You deliberately shut your eyes to what is inevitable, that you may keep in the cabinet some men who are evidently indifferent to the murder, or compulsory flight of all landowners in Ireland . . .'[21]

In the spring of 1881, Smythe was away from the estate. His agent, Sutton, was ill and consequently resigned his position.[22] The local branch of the Land League became involved in the Riggs case, ploughing and sowing his land. Part of the farm was used as a common on which local people grazed their cattle. After Smythe returned Riggs was convicted twice for trespass.[23] In a letter sent to Riggs on 17 November 1881 Smythe obviously was still hoping that Riggs would agree to voluntarily surrender his tenure:

> However though you used about 20 acres of the land without rent, as trespasser, you have still the offer of forgiveness of the debt, and £25 on removal; otherwise prosecution and the enforcement of the decree for cash lent, as well as of that for removal by the sheriff.[24]

His reluctance to evict Riggs may have stemmed to some extent from the long association with the family on the estate. Moreover, he took pride in the fact that he had never evicted a tenant for non-payment of rent during his time as landlord, and was unenthusiastic about taking an action which would sully his reputation in this regard. It is also likely that he was fearful of the consequences of evicting Riggs, as two days later he wrote to Forster suggesting that a military attachment should be sent to Castlepollard.[25] In fact, he remained in regular correspondence with Dublin Castle regarding the 'necessary arrangements in connection with the intended eviction'.[26]

By the spring of 1882, Smythe decided to take action, as he believed that otherwise he was 'becoming guilty of complicity with lawlessness, in allowing so lawless an example to continue in the neighbourhood'.[27] Thus in early March 1882, Smythe notified Riggs in writing, that he was about to be removed, and the eviction duly took place on 18 March. Smythe attended the eviction himself.[28] The newspaper account suggests that it was carried out peacefully by the sub-sheriff who was accompanied by some police and military. After the eviction, Smythe wrote to Riggs and said that he would be paid £10 a year 'as long as no injury was done in consequence of the eviction, and that his life would be insured for £100 for his family'.[29] This is further evidence that Smythe felt some concern regarding the consequences of the eviction, and was taking some precautionary steps to protect himself. On the following Friday, a threatening letter was sent to Smythe's agent.

> This is to warn you to give up immedally Barlow Smyth's agentcy if yo expect to live long let him do his dirty work himself as he is going to be a tyrant the same hand is ready for you as took down Crawford. If you disregard this warning If you mention this letter to any one except your wife you sale your own death warrant I'll hear if you spake of it to peelers or any one else and if I do remember rory death to Tyranny.[30]

As a consequence of this letter, Talbot, Smythe's new agent who had held that position for approximately a month, resigned the following week. Unlike Talbot, Smythe very publicly defied the unofficial defenders of traditional practice by evicting the Riggs family. He directed this action in person, as he later said that he did not wish 'to endanger the life of any subordinate in any degree'.[31] This was compounded twelve days later when Smythe rounded up all the cattle which Riggs had permitted various tenants to graze on the farm and drove them to the pound. The following day, the property was fenced in his presence. On 1 April, the day before the murder, the owners of the cattle were prosecuted at the petty sessions in Collinstown. This would appear to have been the end of the ongoing problems which Richard Riggs had caused Smythe over the previous two years. However, the consequences of the eviction were to plunge Smythe into a whole new set of problems, which were to have a profound effect on the remaining years of his life.

On Saturday 1 April 1882, a group of people from Dublin arrived at Barbavilla House, which is located less than a mile from the village of Collinstown. The house was beautifully situated in a demesne which incorporated formal gardens and extensive woodlands.

It was to this picturesque setting that the party had come to spend Easter in the country. The group comprised of Maria Smythe, married to Smythe's brother Henry, her two daughters, two young gentlemen, and Lady Harriet Monck.[32] The following day was Palm Sunday, and after Sunday service in Collinstown parish church, the brougham carrying Smythe, Maria Smythe and Lady Harriet Monck started off for home, turned into the Barbavilla estate and proceeded up the avenue to a point about 150 yards from the house. Smythe gave the following account of what happened next:

> I was then startled by the noise of glass-breaking, for I hardly realised that a shot had been fired. I suppose I heard the report. I remember I exclaimed, 'Good God, I think we are under fire!' The noise seemed like that of a hailstorm. I then realised we were under fire. At that moment the deceased lady sank forward. I thought she had fainted from terror,

as she was a very nervous person. My attention was diverted from her as I pulled out my revolver, and held it out of the window.[33]

There were four shots in all, but it would seem that the first one was the fatal one. It had entered the carriage through the front glass panels, and struck the back of Maria Smythe's head on the right hand side, shattering her skull. The doctor and police were immediately sent for. On examination of the body, Dr William Carleton, the doctor in Delvin, concluded that the first shot must have killed her instantly on account of the severe damage it inflicted on the brain.

Understandably, the murder had a traumatic effect on Smythe. Firstly, he felt shocked, hurt and angry at the fact that he was the intended victim of the plot, particularly as he perceived himself as being a 'good landlord'. Secondly, Smythe suffered a 'grievous bereavement' on the death of his sister-in-law, Maria, as he had a good relationship with his brother Henry, and his family.[34] Thirdly, he felt bitter and resentful towards the Gladstone administration, which he believed was ultimately responsible for the state of the country and by implication the murder of his sister-in-law. In Smythe's *Tale of Westmeath* he refers to a letter written to the lord lieutenant two hours after the murder.[35] Notwithstanding the shock and bereavement which Smythe had experienced as a result of the murder, the fact that he was capable of sitting down and performing this task given the circumstances, reflects his rather eccentric personality. The following day, he vented his anger in a letter to the prime minister.

> Your practical adhesion to the principle that 'force is no remedy' in the case of Irish savagery, has culminated here in making it easy for the assassin guerrilla of the Land League to murder my sister-in-law, Mrs H. Smythe, yesterday, not long after noonday, in my carriage, returning from church with me (their intended victim) and Lady H. Monck, who also escaped ... I lay the guilt of the deed of blood at your door, in the face of the whole country, supported as you are in that part of your policy by the 'no-rent' M.P.s, their press, and some Irish bishops.[36]

According to Smythe, as the murder took place in broad daylight 'in a populous neighbourhood' the perpetrators in theory would have had to pass several houses to reach the scene of the crime.[37] However, local people with whom the police came into contact were naturally reluctant to provide any information. The correspondent for the *Westmeath Guardian* reported one instance where a local person curtly informed a policeman that he would provide no assistance, as it was up to the constabulary who were paid to do their duty to detect the murderers.[38] No gesture was made on behalf of the tenantry to Smythe, who perceived their silence as approval of 'the deed of blood' and in a letter informed them that they were 'as guilty in God's sight as the murderer'.[39] Smythe received many letters of condolence from outside the parish of Collinstown, but not all of them were sympathetic. An ex-employee wrote from the United States; 'Treat the people better and you'll be treated better yourself'.[40] At the quarter sessions of the grand jury, the county court judge, John Chute Neligan, remarked that although 'every feeling of human nature' was touched by the murder of Maria Smythe, no 'cry of horror had been raised in that district'.[41]

The reaction to the murder from the clergy of the parish provides an interesting contrast. On Easter Sunday, according to a letter written by Smythe to Gladstone, the Catholic clergy of the parish of Collinstown did not condemn the murder or offer public sympathy, but instead issued an invitation to sow the land of a suspect.[42] Smythe's bias must be considered in this instance. On the other hand, the *Westmeath Guardian* reported that at the Church of Ireland Easter vestry, the following resolution was recorded in the minutes:

> . . . we wish to place on record our abhorrence of the atrocious murder which has been perpetrated in our neighbourhood, where Mr Smythe has spent his life, laid out large sums of money, given much employment, always shown a deep interest in each individual and every cause of good . . .[43]

At the Church of Ireland general synod which took place later in April, sympathy was extended to Smythe and his brother and family. The Church of Ireland bishop of Meath, spoke of the privilege of enjoying Smythe's friendship and of his kindly and generous nature. A motion was passed which expressed the synod's 'indignation at the foul deed of assassination'.[44]

Nationally and internationally, the murder created shock waves. The fact that a woman had been murdered accidentally in place of a landlord who had a good reputation, and that it had occurred on a Sunday in broad daylight seemed to be features of this outrage which distinguished it from the many other atrocities which characterised the year 1882. Florence Arnold-Forster's journal recorded the reaction of her father, William Forster, then chief secretary:

> As might be expected, the murder of Mrs Smythe, and all the circumstances attending it, have caused such a thrill of horror and fury as no other outrage has yet done. 'Everyone has gone quite mad over it' says Father, after reading the usually sober columns of the *Irish Times*, 'and I'm sure I am not surprised'.[45]

The *Nation* reported that 'it is needless to say that the event has caused intense excitement and indignation throughout the country'.[46] The 'presumption that the murderous missile found an unintended billet deepens the gloom and sadness of the awful occurrence while it in no way mitigates the crime or lessens the guilt of the assassin,' wrote the *Freeman's Journal*. The same paper also commented that 'the course pursued by a misguided knot – for we cannot believe the murderers to be more numerous – is one which will alienate from Ireland home and foreign sympathy'.[47] Smythe, who bought the *Freeman's Journal*, wrote a letter to the editor in response to this article and informed him:

Your wretched article of Tuesday affects to denounce the murder. Why? Because it was of an innocent lady, by an unintended bullet! and by a misguided knot because you cannot believe the murderers to be more numerous! ... Misguided knot! – a large knot indeed extended to most parts of this miserable island where I have passed my long life, doing my best according to my light.

The tone of the letter captures the depth of anger and sorrow which Smythe was experiencing during the aftermath of the murder. As in the letter to Gladstone where he blamed the Liberal administration, he likewise perceived the material published in the *Freeman's Journal* as a contributory factor in the murder: 'Your wicked suggestive weekly lying cartoons have helped to this deed of blood, misleading further those ready to be misled'.[48] According to a telegraph sent from Rome to the editor of the *Evening Telegraph*, 'Mrs Smythe's murder produced a profound sensation in the Vatican and the Propaganda'.[49] Cowper, then lord lieutenant, wrote a short note to Smythe expressing his 'feelings of horror and commiseration' and a few days later wrote to enquire after the health of Lady Monck, on behalf of the Queen.[50]

One of the immediate consequences for the tenants on the Barbavilla estate was that within a week of the murder, Smythe employed the services of a non-resident agent 'who can make no further allowances, nor do anything on the property not strictly required by law'.[51] Shortly afterwards Smythe emigrated to Britain, a move which he described as 'having to fly, under escort, from my ancient home for endeavouring to vindicate the right of property in a single case undeniably just and exceptionally defensible in every point ...'.[52] From this point onwards relations between Smythe and his tenants were placed on a strictly formal basis. The newly appointed agent was Matthew Weld O'Connor of Baltrasna House, County Meath, an unpopular choice from the point of view of the tenants, on account of his reputation for ruthlessness. Weld O'Connor had attracted the attention of the Land League earlier on during 1880 when a number of meetings were held in the Mountnugent area to protest against his action as land agent.

The influx of extra police into the Collinstown area was another outcome of the murder. On the day following the murder, they arrested Richard Riggs, his wife, Rose, and their son, Philip, and remanded them in custody for eight days.[53] Rev. John Curry, parish priest in Collinstown later became involved in a campaign to reopen the case of the Barbavilla prisoners and published a pamphlet regarding the trials. In this publication, he referred to the efforts of local police sergeant, Thomas Lynch, who tried 'to get people to swear to his suggestions under promises of reward and under threats of getting them seriously into trouble'. In fact, the parishioners were 'cautioned from the altar against telling lies for him, so notorious were his disreputable efforts to trump up a case against someone'.[54] This 'cautioning' had been carried out by Curry's predecessor, Rev. Luke Farrelly.[55] Although Curry's pamphlet has a decidedly anti-police bias, other sources would support this view.[56] Not only were additional police uncomfortable for the local community, but expensive. This cost was met by a tax which was levied on the ratepayers in the baronies of Delvin and Fore. By 30 May 1882, Smythe added a further £300 to the reward of £2,000 which had been issued by the government 'in the case of the horrible murder'. In the notice printed on the front of the *Westmeath Guardian*, Smythe outlined the facts of the case regarding Riggs's eviction and concluded that '... these facts proving that the Collinstown conspirators, who have terrorised the country must be the instruments of men averse to all rights of ownership however fairly exercised, and the enemies of every landlord as much as of myself'.[57]

Under the supervision of the Fore branch of the Ladies' Land League, a wooden house was built in Gilliardstown to house the five members of the Riggs family who had been evicted. These pre-fabricated wooden huts had begun to appear throughout the country in October 1881 to house evicted tenants. They were approximately 20 feet long, with windows and wooden floors, and a galvanised roof.[58] A stove for heating and cooking was also provided. In fact, the subject of this hut was raised in the house of commons during the second week of July in 1882.

> Mr Tottenham asked the chief secretary to the lord lieutenant of Ireland whether he state to the house the reasons which had induced the lord lieutenant to permit the erection of a Land League hut near Collinstown, Westmeath, on the boundary of Mr Smythe's property ... and whether he would inform the house what arrangements had been made to prevent intimidation arising from the erection of such a hut.[59]

The choice of location, the townland of Gilliardstown, was significant in terms of landlord-tenant-relations in Collinstown, as it was here that the Collinstown and Fore branch of the Land League had clashed with Thomas Ellis, who acted as agent for his brother, Robert, over the refusal to grant abatements. Not only was the selection of the site in Gilliardstown provocative, the erection of this building communicated a message of defiance to the local landlord community. Just how potent a symbol of intimidation it represented to local landlords and agents is evident in the various correspondence it generated with Dublin Castle. In October 1882, Thomas Ellis stated in a deposition that he believed that the presence of the hut would prevent the surrounding tenantry from paying rents and that, from experience, even visiting the lands in an attempt to make arrangements, was at risk to his life.[60] Butler, who was a special resident magistrate, sought advice from the law adviser in Dublin Castle, whether or not it would be wise for Ellis to proceed with a case against Riggs, forcing him to remove the hut on the grounds that it was a source of intimidation. The response from Dublin Castle was that he should not continue with the case:

It must be borne in mind that prosecuting a person for intimidation where the intimidation charged was in the erection of a dwelling place where the person charged resides or is sheltered is pushing the law to a very extreme and dangerous limit.[61]

Smythe, now living in Ilfracombe, Devon, also was in communication with Dublin Castle about this hut, which he referred to as 'a monument of outrage'. He was incensed that a year after the murder it still was allowed to remain beside his property, 'within two miles of the scene of the murder as well as that of the eviction'.[62] The failure on the part of the authorities to remove the hut indicated to Smythe that it was 'deliberately sanctioned by the special resident magistrate'. When this was put to Butler, the magistrate in question, he haughtily replied: 'When Mr Smythe says that the Land League hut was deliberately sanctioned by the special resident magistrate, he not only states what is false, but what he well knows to be false'.[63]

The eviction and murder which occurred in Collinstown in the spring of 1882, bore many of the hallmarks of the traditional method of defending the 'customary agrarian code'. After the murder, the wall of silence facing the police investigating the murder was also a typical communal reaction to an agrarian crime. Did this indicate a consensus among the tenant community that they supported the plan to murder Smythe, or did their non-co-operation stem from intimidation? It is clearly difficult to evaluate the degree to which the actual murder was approved of. What the available sources indicate more clearly is that the aftermath presented an opportunity for the tenants to affirm their anti-landlordism. This was manifested in the lack of condolences to Smythe, the non-co-operation with the police and the building of the wooden hut for the Riggs family. Intimidation cannot be ruled out as a deterministic element either; if a tenant were known to be an informer, for instance, he or she was likely to be the subject of victimisation. Smythe's behaviour in the context of the eviction and the murder signify the complex personality of this landlord. He sought publicity for the Riggs case to justify his own action in the eviction and more broadly to highlight the shortcomings of the Liberal administration, and yet did so, it would appear, fully aware of the potential danger it involved with regard to his own safety. In terms of estate management he reacted to the murder by distancing himself from the tenant community. Thus he moved to Britain, employed a non-resident agent and thereafter maintained more formal relations with his tenants.

The Aftermath of the Murder, 1882–5

A week after the murder, a body of police from Mullingar arrested six men on a charge of being connected with the murder of Mrs Smythe: Arthur Swords, Joseph McGrath, Michael McGrath, William Boyhan, John Gill, and Patrick Fagan. Patrick Hanlon, who admitted being in Barbavilla wood at the time of the murder, was arrested shortly afterwards.[1] Following the release of these men eight days later, one of the group, Joseph McGrath, began providing information regarding the murder to the sergeant in Collinstown.[2] According to local oral testimony the sergeant frequently called to the McGrath household at night in order to interview McGrath.[3] His role as informer is confirmed by a report sent by Special Resident Magistrate Butler to the chief secretary informing him that the police received 'positive information that a man named William Boyhan was selected by lot by a secret association to be one of the murderers, and that he was one of the persons who fired the shots at the carriage'.[4] According to the same report, there was evidence that Boyhan was close to the scene of the outrage and had been charged with the murder and remanded in custody from time to time.[5] However, this arrangement took an unexpected turn when Joseph McGrath 'who had given the constabulary most useful information, and on whom they mainly relied to enable them to bring the crime home to Boyhan' became ill with scarlet fever and died on 15 May 1882.[6] Boyhan had to be discharged due to lack of evidence on 20 May and two days later he set sail for the United States.[7] Additional information which had been given to Captain Butler indicated that a meeting had taken place in Byrne's public house, in Collinstown, on the night before the murder.

However, in spite of this promising start, the murder investigation made little or no headway until April 1883. According to a report in the *Westmeath Examiner* on 7 April 1883, approximately seventy witnesses were examined at the investigation which had taken place in Collinstown. Although no arrests were made, it was believed that 'very important evidence was adduced'.[8] Tensions were obviously running high in the area, as evidenced by an article entitled 'Seeking Evidence' which featured in the *Westmeath Examiner* on 5 May 1883. This alleged that a man, who lived near Collinstown was visited by a detective and the head constable from a neighbouring station and interrogated about his whereabouts on the day of the Barbavilla murder. The man's identity was not disclosed:

His answers not being to the satisfaction of the 'detectives' one of them clenching his fist and calling him a puppy and informed him the day would come when he would be glad like some of the rest to get leave to give an account but that he would not be let. The interview concluded with the detective saying to the man 'You spent the day with the murderer'.[9]

Although the nationalist ethos of the *Westmeath Examiner* must be taken into account here, it nevertheless reveals that people were being subjected to pressure in order to secure information and in addition that the police themselves were under pressure to secure a conviction.

Two witnesses emerged from the investigation which had taken place in Collinstown. Although they were father and son and one lived in Clonmel, County Tipperary, and the other in Castlepollard, County Westmeath, they claimed to have provided depositions independently of each other during the months of May, June and July 1883. Their evidence was of major significance in effecting the convictions of a group of men who became known as the Barbavilla prisoners. Although other witnesses took the stand and two of the prisoners became crown witnesses or 'approvers', it was the information which the McKeons provided which formed the basis of the case for the crown. The chief baron drew the jury's attention to this fact in his summary:

> If the jury believed beyond all reasonable doubt that in substance the McKeons were telling the truth they would have to convict the prisoners, but if they believed that the McKeons were engaged in a conspiracy to take away the liberties of the prisoners, or that a solid and reasonable doubt existed in their minds as to their guilt, a verdict of acquittal should be returned.[10]

Patrick McKeon senior was a carpenter who lived and worked in Castlepollard, three miles from the village of Collinstown. His father, a native of Kilpatrick, had the following to say about his son: 'Since he was a boy of sixteen years of age he was nothing but a drunkard, a vagabond and a rogue; in fact he could not get too bad a character'.[11] The second witness was the old man's twenty-year old grandson who had joined the army in February 1883 and was stationed in the barracks in Clonmel. Prior to this he had been apprenticed as a blacksmith to John Walshe of Ballyknock, close to the Barbavilla demesne, where he was working during the spring of 1882. Head Constable Lynch who had spent nine and a half years in Collinstown, described him during one of the trials as 'a wild young boy'.[12] On at least one occasion, he had been in jail on charges of breaking into a house and stealing various items. On entering the army he deserted his wife and lied about his apprenticeship to Walshe.[13]

The McKeons' evidence centred around two pivotal issues: the movement of a group of men on the day of the murder and a meeting which was alleged to have taken place outside Fagan's house in Kilpatrick at which the murder was planned. McKeon junior had provided three depositions relating to the day of the murder.[14] A comparison of the three depositions reveals many inconsistencies in the details he provided relating to the murder. For example, on 17 May in his first deposition he stated that on the morning of the murder he observed Robert Elliott, a journeyman blacksmith with whom he was working, with a revolver in his pocket. Later that afternoon he observed Elliott again changing the revolver from one pocket to another.[15] In the second deposition taken on 20 June, he stated that he saw Elliott on the morning in question with a cut down gun or a long pistol which was projecting from under his coat. McKeon was known to carry a revolver himself, and would thus be familiar with the relevant terminology.[16] McKeon's deposition was followed immediately by the first wave of arrests. At the subsequent trials his information regarding the day of the murder was to influence the structure the case was to assume. On account of the number of prisoners who were eventually arrested, they were tried in two groups. The indictment against all of the prisoners was the same: that on the 24 March 1882, 'they unlawfully did conspire, combine, confederate, and agree together, feloniously, wilfully, and of their malice aforethought, to kill and murder one William Barlow Smythe'.[17] There had been insufficient evidence to charge any of the prisoners with the actual murder.[18]

However, the evidence provided by McKeon junior in relation to the day of the murder suggested that the men who were involved in its perpetration

3. The Barbavilla prisoners, back row (left to right): Robert Elliott, Bryan Fitzpatrick, John Boyhan, James Gaffney. Front row: Bernard Rynne, Patrick Fagan, John Fagan and Pat Hanlon. These men were arrested in the first wave of arrests. Pat Hanlon later became a crown witness and was discharged. (Source: *Weekly Freeman*, 10 July 1883)

were Robert Elliott, Arthur Swords, Michael McGrath, Bernard Rynne and Bryan Fitzpatrick and these prisoners formed the first group to be tried. Subsequently they were found guilty and sentenced to the severest sentence the law imposed for conspiracy to murder – ten years' penal servitude.[19]

McKeon senior's information was described as 'startling evidence' in the *Westmeath Guardian* when it came to light in court on 20 June 1883.[20] It concerned a meeting which was alleged to have taken place in the farmyard outside the Widow Fagan's house in Kilpatrick on 24 March 1882. According to his information, three of the Dublin Invincibles came down to Collinstown to start an 'Assassination society', which was aimed at removing 'tyrants'.[21] One of these men was Michael Fagan, a son of the Widow Fagan's. His brother John, and William Boyhan were also present, both of whom had left for the United States.[22] Another person named was Joseph McGrath who had died in the meantime.[23] McKeon listed a number of other local men in attendance, some of whom were already in prison. According to his statement, the people present formed a circle and a book was passed around to be sworn upon by those intent upon joining. Four people refused to swear on the book, among these were the two McKeons. A number of local 'tyrants' were listed for removal: William Barlow Smythe, Matthew Weld O'Connor, William Edward Smyth of Glananea, Lord Longford, and Mr Keating of Newcastle. Arrangements for the murder of Mr Smythe were made with a select group, a signalman was appointed and afterwards another meeting was planned to take place in the house of Bryan Fitzpatrick's father.[24] McKeon reported that this meeting did not in fact take place, instead it was held outside Byrne's public house, Collinstown, the night before the murder.

This new evidence must be examined within the context of the other revelations which came to light in Dublin during the spring of 1883. From late January, there was widespread publicity regarding the group of men who had been arrested in connection with the Phoenix Park murders, in among them Michael Fagan from Kilpatrick.[25] When a number of the prisoners became crown witnesses and supplied information for the prosecution in the months that followed, the plot to kill the chief secretary and the under secretary unfolded, causing a sensation in the Irish, British and American press. The ritual of the swearing in of new members while passing a book around described by McKeon senior was reminiscent of the Invincible ritual of taking an oath over a pen knife. The appointment of a signalman likewise was another common factor. More importantly, it was the phrase 'the removal of tyrants' as the object of the society which had a very familiar ring as these words had been repeat-edly featured in newspaper reports on the Invincible trials.

Although McKeon alleged his son was at this meeting, there was no mention of it in his son's deposition which had been made over two weeks earlier. In fact, in McKeon junior's second deposition made on 27 June, he merely stated that he was at the Widow Fagan's the Friday week before the murder – there was no reference to Invincibles or any other details. By the time McKeon junior made his third deposition on 17 July, he included all the details of the meeting which had featured in his father's statement. Unsurprisingly, the omission of the meeting in Fagan's in the first deposition was utilised by Dr Boyd, one of the lawyers representing the prisoners:

> Dr Boyd, QC Was it a mistake for you to leave out all mention of your being at Widow Fagan's on the 24th [March 1882] in your first information? (No answer.)
>
> Was it a mistake of you to leave all mention of the meeting of the 24th in your last information? Don't speak so fast. I can't understand you properly.
>
> Does the witness pledge his oath to that. Was it a mistake of you to leave all mention of the meeting out of your first information? Is that slow enough for you? (No answer).[26]

Another curious aspect about the evidence regarding the meeting outside Fagan's house was that although McKeon senior provided this deposition on 5 June, arrests were not carried out the following day as had happened following his son's information. In addition, there was no mention of the meeting when the prisoners were brought into court again on 13 June 1883 and further remanded. McKeon's evidence was not used in court until 20 June, and the arrests which it brought about were not carried out until 5 July. It is difficult to account for this delayed response on the part of the police. Curry argued that the delay was deliberate in order to afford McKeon junior an opportunity to memorise the facts of the meeting which his father described in his deposition. This would suggest that the McKeons were given the opportunity to become familiar with each other's evidence, although at the trials the prosecution repeatedly emphasised that they had not been in communication with each other since the night of the meeting at the Widow Fagan's. It is fair to say that this absence of communication was pivotal in the whole case. During the trials Judge Lawson drew attention to the importance of this fact: 'To insinuate that the McKeons had interviews [with each other] while in the hands of the police is to insinuate that the very sources of justice are polluted'.[27] However, Curry investigated this aspect of the evidence and in his pamphlet provided a written statement of a sergeant who saw the two McKeons together at a police station in Dublin with Sergeant Lynch.[28] Maurice Fitzgerald, the sergeant in question, alleged that he was told by Lynch on this occasion that McKeon senior had expressly come up to Dublin from Castlepollard to talk to the son about the evidence: 'Let me talk to him and it will be all right' he is reputed to have said.[29] A juror who convicted the prisoners later wrote to Curry:

I would have no hesitation in stating that I would have acquitted the prisoners if it had been proved on their behalf that the McKeons had an opportunity of communication with one another while in the hands of the police.[30]

The same juror also recalled that Sergeant Lynch had 'denied positively that they had met and communicated'.[31] If the jury believed this were true, they would have been more willing to give the McKeons the benefit of the doubt when glaring inconsistencies in their depositions became apparent as the trials dragged on. Given the personalities of these two crown witnesses, the inconsistencies in their depositions and the obviously contrived elements in their evidence, it is difficult on balance to accept their credibility. This is compounded by Fitzgerald's information about the McKeons' meeting in Dublin. The fact that they had access to each other's evidence is clearly borne out by the changes which they made to their depositions during their time in police custody. Finally, the fact that they claimed to have been present at the meeting in Fagan's yard, refused to be 'sworn in' and yet were permitted to remain and become privy to the details of the murder conspiracy, casts further doubt on the veracity of their evidence. In discussing the factors which motivated the McKeons to be willing to provide information to the police, the lure of the huge reward must be considered. County Westmeath, according to one report was 'strewn thickly with proclamations announcing the immense reward that was offered for information by the authorities'.[32] Also noteworthy is the fact that the deadline for providing information and receiving the reward was 28 May 1883, eleven days after McKeon junior's first deposition.

Twelve prisoners were finally committed for trial on 22 July 1883. The group, which ranged from labourers to substantial farmers, was representative of the tenant community in Collinstown (See table 1).

William McCormack, the treasurer of the local branch of the Land League, had a holding of approximately 400 acres, and L'Estrange was described as being 'comfortably off'.[33] Patrick Cole had a farm of fifty acres as well as being a shopkeeper and a poor law guardian. The *Irish Times* reporting on the arrests noted that there 'was much excitement in the neighbourhood on account of the respectability of some of the prisoners'.[34] On the other end of the spectrum were Bernard Rynne, a labourer, and Robert Elliott, a travelling blacksmith. The range of society represented by the prisoners was one of the points underlined by T.H. Teeling, the solicitor defending Elliott later on at the trials in Dublin. He pointed out the close resemblance to this case and that of the Phoenix Park murders trials: the Phoenix Park prisoners had 'James Carey, town councillor, at one end and Joe Brady, the bricklayer at the other'.[35] The Barbavilla trials also had 'station and respectability on one hand' represented by William McCormack and 'lowliness or humility of position on the other' as represented by Robert Elliott.[36] Teeling was using this

Table 1. Arrests made 18 May–5 July 1883

NAME	ADDRESS	OCCUPATION
John Boyhan	Kilpatrick	stonemason
Michael McGrath	Rickardstown	Not specified
Arthur Swords	Rickardstown	farmer
Bryan Fitzpatrick	Tuitestown	labourer
John Fagan	Collinstown	John Talbot's servant
Patrick Fagan	Monkstown	Not specified
Robert Elliott	No fixed abode	journeyman blacksmith
James Gaffney	Kilpatrick	labourer
Patrick Cole	Kilpatrick	shopkeeper and farmer
Michael L'Estrange	Kilpatrick	farmer
William McCormack	Ballnavine	farmer
John McGrath	Collinstown	farmer
Bernard Rynne	Kilpatrick	labourer

(Sources: *Westmeath Guardian*, 18 May; 6 Jul. 1883; Joseph Wade's notes, Westmeath County Library; Richard Griffith, *General valuation of rateable property in Ireland, counties of Meath and Westmeath, valuation of the several tenements in the union of Castletowndelvin situated in the counties above named* (Dublin, 1854), pp 23–77)

similarity to illustrate that the conspiracy had 'its origin in the brain of the McKeons' and that they had a ready-made pattern in the Phoenix Park case.[37]

It is interesting to note that the McKeons had grievances against some of the people they claimed were present at the meeting. Patrick Cole remarked later on that he could not understand why his name was associated with this meeting and could only account for it by the fact that McKeon had 'an old spleen' against him.[38] McCormack was alleged to have prevented McKeon senior from getting employment and that the latter said 'he would catch him for it some day'.[39] Robert Elliott stated that he was fearful for his life in the presence of McKeon junior and would not remain alone with him in Walshe's forge.[40] If the meeting were conjured up, the fact that there existed a history of ill feeling between the McKeons and some of the prisoners would help to explain why they chose to name these people as members of the group who attended the meeting on 24 March 1882. Others named by the McKeons such as Michael McGrath, Patrick Fagan and Arthur Swords, had been among the group arrested by the police shortly after the murder which would account for the fact that their names were included.

The prisoners were first detained in Mullingar jail. During that time the members of the press were the only 'outside public' which were permitted to attend court hearings.[41] Nevertheless, friends and family of the prisoners demonstrated their support by greeting the prisoners outside, for instance, the *Westmeath Examiner* reported that the 'street leading from the jail to the courthouse was thronged with the friends of the prisoners' on the day the prisoners were committed for trial.[42] It was also reported that a 'warm shaking of hands and wild lamentation' took place *en route*.[43] Concern for plight of the prisoners' families prompted Rev. Luke Farrelly, the Roman Catholic parish priest in Collinstown, and his curate, Rev. Daniel Cuskelly, to write a letter to the *Westmeath Examiner* which was published on 14 July 1883. They proposed opening a subscription list in the column of the *Westmeath Examiner* to enable 'the charitably disposed' to come to the assistance of the prisoners' families.[44] This fund continued until 16 February 1884 and realised £49.17s.7d. in that time, which would be the equivalent of £39,191 in the 1990s. Subscribers to the Barbavilla prisoners' fund had their name and subscription printed in the *Westmeath Examiner*. The structure of its presentation is interesting in that it reflects the various strata of society – it was always in descending order based on the amount of the subscription. It is significant that 67.7 per cent of the individual donations listed were subscriptions of five shillings or less, reflecting the degree of support from the poorer people in the area. One option open to people who could not afford to send a subscription to the newspaper – the lowest denomination donated was one shilling of which there were many – was to buy raffle tickets which sold at six pence each. A raffle for a silver watch was held in Fore between the months of September and November for the benefit of the fund, and realised £2. 6s. 0d.[45] Some individuals such as John Dunlevey and James Bacon organised a collection in the townland of Benison Lodge and the nearby parish of Whitehall.[46] The stewards at the races at Moortown collected £5 in September.[47] William Gaffney, a native of Mullingar living in Liverpool, subscribed £1 and in a letter addressed to the editor expressed hope that people of Mullingar would subscribe generously to the fund, and 'thus return their answer to the government for the manner in which they have arrested and treated respectable citizens'.[48] In fact, few if any subscriptions came from Mullingar. The list would suggest that support mainly came from the people in the parish of Collinstown, and neighbouring parishes.

Support for the prisoners manifested itself through another channel. In August 1883, a vacancy occurred on the board of guardians for the Poor Law Union of Delvin due to the death of Robert McCormack of Glenidan, who represented the Fore East division of the union. The popular choice for a replacement was one of the prisoners, William McCormack, who was still in Mullingar prison at that time.[49] McCormack was returned unopposed, and the *Westmeath Examiner* interpreted his nomination as 'a protest against the action of the government in arresting and keeping in prison himself and his fellow prisoners on the testimony of informers'.[50] Although the pro-nationalist bias of newspaper cannot be disregarded, the gesture nevertheless signified unequivocal support for McCormack and the prisoners. In a broader context, McCormack's election may be viewed as part of the movement of the Irish party to promote the appointment of tenants as officers on the boards of poor law guardians during the years 1879–86. These boards served important local government functions. By 1886, the Poor Law Union of Delvin, according to Feingold's study of the subject, was among the radical unions throughout the country which had no landowners among the officers. Feingold argued that such unions were 'controlled entirely by that element which represented the tenant electorate'.[51]

Of the seven prisoners in the second group: John McGrath, John Fagan, Patrick Fagan, John Boyhan, James Gaffney, William McCormack and Patrick Cole, only six appeared in the dock on 9 June 1884.[52] The crown had accepted one of the prisoners as an 'approver'. This was Patrick Cole, the farmer, shop-keeper, and poor law guardian from Kilpatrick.[53] Cole's statement included new material on nationalist speeches made by Curley and McCaffrey which, as Curry observed, 'were made as if reporters were present'.[54] New names were included such as Pat Fitzsimons and William Woods.[55] Cole also confessed to being a fenian, but had not attended a meeting for about eight years.[56] He projected an image of participating in the meeting at the Widow Fagan's reluctantly, because from experience he was fearful of the consequences of not rejoining.[57] Not only did the conspiracy meeting feature in Cole's information, but also the movement of the first group of prisoners on the day of the murder.

Cole's evidence was an important determinant in securing the convictions of the second group of prisoners. Hitherto, the only evidence of the meeting in Fagan's yard was the information in the McKeons' depositions. The outcome was that five men were sentenced to seven years of penal servitude and one prisoner, John McGrath, was sentenced to twelve months. Why he received a more lenient sentence is unclear. Curry suggested that it was because he paid his rent when the 'no rent manifesto' was issued, unlike the other prisoners.[58] This may have been an advantage to McGrath, but what would seem a more likely explanation is the fact that it emerged in court that he was a 'simple-minded fellow'. In fact he had been in the lunatic asylum in Mullingar for a period of six or seven months, twenty years earlier according to his brother Christopher.[59] Cole's information was effective in allaying any lingering doubts the jury may have harboured regarding the genuineness of the McKeons' statements. The apparent sincerity which characterised his testimony gave it an air of convincing authenticity. The political nature of the crime was emphasised on account of the speeches which he deposed were delivered at the meeting and his admission of his own connection with fenianism. All of these factors combined to strengthen the case of the crown, but understandably had a very damaging effect on Cole's standing in the community from this point onwards.

The Prevention of Crime (Ireland) Act passed in 1882 contained a clause whereby the attorney general or defendant, may require a case to be heard by a jury of special jurors in another county.[60] Thus the Barbavilla prisoners were tried in Green Street in Dublin, instead of County Westmeath. This had major implications for the prisoners and indeed other cases such as the prisoners tried for the Maamtrasna murders.[61] Of the 200 jurors who made up the panel from which the jury was selected, 194 could be challenged by the crown as opposed to six by the prisoners. Relating to the trials of the Barbavilla prisoners, the *Freeman's Journal* noted on 14 February 1884 that '25 Roman Catholic jurors of the city and county, some of whom were gentlemen of the highest standing, and at least one a magistrate of the county in Dublin' were asked to stand aside, and eventually 'twelve good and true non-Catholic jurors were empanelled'.[62] The social composition of the jury selected in the trials had major implications for the prisoners particularly as the prosecution emphasised the involvement of some of the prisoners in the local Land League, deliberately playing upon the prejudices of the class and religion of the majority of jurors. For example, attention was focused on the fact that William McCormack was treasurer of the local branch of the Land League and that his sister, Rebecca, was treasurer of the local Ladies' Land League.[63] Where it was appropriate the defence also took advantage of anti-Land League prejudice: Dr Webb Q.C. defending John McGrath emphasised the fact that he was neither 'a Land Leaguer, nor an Invincible, nor a Fenian'.[64] The appointment of a special jury in another county came about as a result of the 'the growing conviction within the Irish administration that additional measures would be necessary to bring those guilty of crime within the reach of the law'.[65] By the autumn of 1882, for instance, there had been sixty murders committed in succession which had remained unsolved.[66] Thus it could be argued that the Prevention of Crime Act in 1882 which was enacted in order to address this problem of unpunished crime, in fact over-compensated, providing circumstances which did not lend themselves to a fair trial.

When Patrick Cole returned to Kilpatrick he was faced with a difficult readjustment process. By the time the final convictions were made he had been in jail for almost a year. When he rejoined his family, protection had to be provided for him, on account of his becoming an informant. He obviously had difficulty in finding labourers who were prepared to work for him, and there is evidence to suggest that outside labourers were provided by the Property Defence Association.[67] This organisation was the collective response of the landlords to the Land League. It provided assistance at evictions, sheriffs' sales and in some cases where boycotting was in operation. Men employed by this association were called 'Emergency men'. In early September 1884, during a week of special devotions in the Catholic church in Collinstown, Rev. John Curry, the newly appointed parish priest, received a message from Jane Cole – wife of Patrick Cole – requesting an interview. This was granted and Cole made a statement in the presence of two priests, stating that the evidence given by her husband was 'concocted by him to satisfy the crown and to save himself'. She knew that he believed that the meeting in Fagan's yard which the McKeons described never took place.[68] On the following Sunday, Patrick Cole came to the sacristy of the church, accompanied by police, and also made a statement.[69]

In consideration for his seven young children who would have become 'utterly destitute' had he been convicted, he had become an informant. At first, when he had agreed to give information, he had made a statement which was rejected 'inasmuch as it contained no information regarding the alleged meeting at the Widow Fagan's'. He continued:

> I was further told by Head-Constable Lynch that "unless I made a clean breast of it" and told all about that meeting, my evidence would not be taken. I subsequently made the statement which I afterwards swore to on two trials. I now declare that evidence was untrue, except as regards my connection with fenianism many years ago. I swore to what was false when I said I attended a meeting at the Widow Fagan's. I never knew of such a meeting. I don't believe such a meeting was held. I had no personal knowledge of any meeting in or about Byrne's publichouse though I swore I attended one there.[70]

Cole's admission not only undermined the evidence given by the McKeons, but also threw the manner in which the case was conducted open to question, especially regarding the role played by Sergeant Lynch. If Lynch manipulated Cole in this manner, there was a strong possibility that he had acted in this way with other witnesses. As a result of the Coles' interviews, Curry decided in September 1884, to take up the cause of the Barbavilla prisoners. His decision to go to the local members of parliament for assistance rather than to church leaders stemmed from the outcome of the Maamtrasna case where the archbishop of Tuam's request to grant 'a proper inquiry' was refused by the government. Both members of parliament for Westmeath, Sullivan and Harrington, pledged their support and indeed Sullivan spent a few days in the locality and became 'convinced that a gross miscarriage of justice had taken place in the case'.[71] In addition, both M.P.s endorsed a letter sent by Curry to the lord lieutenant, Earl Spencer, in November 1884, which requested that the case be reopened, and that Cole's confession not merely justified but demanded a revision of the trials.[72] A reply from the lord lieutenant's secretary on 23 December 1884, stated that apart from the alleged statement of Cole, there was nothing new 'affecting the accuracy of the case' and that no sufficient reasons existed for a further inquiry into the case.[73] In March 1885, Curry decided to publish a pamphlet compiled of the 'evidence and circumstances bearing upon the guilt or innocence of the Barbavilla prisoners' hoping to arouse public opinion on their behalf.[74] A copy of the pamphlet was sent to Parnell who acknowledged it in a short letter on 7 June 1885 in which he assured Curry that he would use his 'best exertions on behalf of the Barbavilla prisoners upon every possible occasion'.[75]

Such an occasion arose the following month on 17 July in the house of commons. During a debate Parnell called the attention of the house to the 'maladministration of the criminal law in Ireland' and to move

> that in the opinion of this house, it is the duty of the government to institute strict enquiry into the evidence and convictions in the Maamtrasna, Barbavilla, Crossmaglen and Castleisland cases, the case of the brothers Delahunty and generally all the cases in which witnesses examined in the trials now declare they committed perjury, or in which proof of the innocence of the accused is tendered by credible persons.[76]

Parnell observed that as there had been a change of government he hoped that justice would be done in the above cases. Since the fall of the Liberal party from power in June, overtures had been made by the Conservatives towards the Irish party. In the spring of 1885, several Tories had begun to discuss the concept of peasant proprietorship and by June 1885 the Irish party had good reason to consider their proposals favourably.[77] However, the Conservative response to Parnell's motion was defensive rather than supportive and Parnell was requested to withdraw the motion. As Comerford notes: 'asking one administration to reopen its predecessor's business was a violation of unwritten laws and precedents'.[78] Unwilling to upset any political apple carts, Parnell reacted to the Conservative response by withdrawing the motion. However, the chancellor of the exchequer, Hicks Beach, had left an opening as far as the prisoners in the various cases were concerned:

> The present lord lieutenant ... had authorised me to state that if memorials are presented of statements made to him on behalf of those referred to in this motion they will be considered by him with the same personal attention which he would feel himself bound to give to all cases, great or small ...[79]

Curry took his cue from this speech and sent a memorial to Lord Carnarvon on 24 July 1885. He included printed extracts from his publications on the subject beseeching Carnarvon to pay close attention to the whole case, and believing that when he does, he will 'speedily liberate ten men unjustly convicted on a concocted charge'.[80]

The local community was hopeful of a positive outcome. On 4 September 1885, a resolution was passed by the Delvin board of poor law guardians which stated that not only was a full investigation necessary in the interest of justice, but also in the interest of the ratepayers of the union 'who have suffered by the unjust incarceration of many of the prisoners, some of whose friends [family members] are inmates of the workhouse'. In addition, the guardians were concerned that the evidence of McKeon junior should be investigated as he had 'deserted his wife and left her chargeable on the union and shortly afterwards perjured himself by enlisting as a single man'.[81]

After a delay of four months, Curry received a terse reply on 2 November 1885 from the assistant under-secretary which affirmed that the case would not be reviewed. The lord lieutenant had considered the case and concluded that 'there had not been a failure of justice'. Curry wrote another and final letter on 15 November that informed Carnarvon that he did not believe his memorial received 'either fair or full consideration'.[82] In the light of all the new information he now had at hand, Curry was convinced that the case could not have been adequately reviewed 'without asking a single question, without inspecting a single document, without examining a single witness'.[83] For example, one of the items which had come into Curry's possession since the trials was an account book which proved that Patrick McKeon senior was in Castlepollard on the night of the alleged meeting in Fagan's.[84] It recorded that he was working for Brogan his employer, on the evening of the 24 March 1882.[85] A memorial which included among its signatures four M.P.s: Sullivan, Gill, Harrington and Tuite testified that they had inspected the document and believed it to be authentic 'and had it been produced and fully explained to the juries they could not have convicted the prisoners'.[86]

Cole's admission of perjury a few months after the trials ended and the sense of injustice in the Barbavilla case which Curry believed it revealed were important in motivating him to become active on behalf of the prisoners. His efforts were described by a local person in a letter to the *Westmeath Examiner* as 'Father Curry's laudable exertions to have the poor men pining away innocently in penal servitude restored to their sorrowing families'.[87] He invested considerable time and energy into his attempts to have the case reopened and clearly utilised the avenues which were open to him to the maximum. In his final letter to Carnarvon, his frustration with the response from Dublin Castle is apparent in the closing lines, when he affirms that he looked forward to the time when the Barbavilla prisoners would be set free 'after being too long the victims of an abominable law and of a still more abominable administration'.[88]

Curry was very scathing about what he believed was the connection forced by the police between the Barbavilla case and the Invincibles, as he wrote to Carnarvon:

> The Phoenix Park trials were then before the public. An unfortunate convict in them – Michael Fagan – had his friends living here, and the bright idea came into the sergeant's mind that a meeting of Invincibles at Fagan's house would be just the thing to accuse the prisoners of.[89]

However, there are grounds to believe that there was a connection between the Invincibles and the Barbavilla murder. The reminiscences of John Mallon, the detective who was in charge of the investigation into the Phoenix Park murders, were serialised over a couple of months in *Lloyd's Weekly News* in 1909. In one of the articles, Mallon claims that only two crimes outside Dublin could be connected with the Invincibles: the Barbavilla and Loughrea

murders.[90] The latter occurred on 9 June 1882. Blake, the agent of Lord
Clanrickarde, was driving to Mass in Loughrea, County Galway, with his wife
and servant when two shots were fired from behind a wall killing Blake and his
driver instantly.[91] In a book of Mallon's reminiscences written by Frederick
Muir Bussy, but reputed to have been on an 'as told to' basis, Mallon remarked
that the weapons used in both the above murders were 'far different to those that
might be expected to be in the possession of ordinary peasants for the purpose
of scaring crows'.[92] Mallon traced the source of these weapons: they had come
via Dublin through Dan Curley, one of the Invincibles who was a native of
Loughrea. Some of them were transferred by Caffrey, another Invincible, to
Loughrea, while others were taken down to Barbavilla by Fagan.[93] Regarding
Michael Fagan and the Barbavilla murder, Bussy wrote: '. . . Mallon affirms that
there is no shadow of a doubt that Fagan not only superintended the "removal"
of Mrs Smythe, but actually used one of the rifles'.[94]

The late Leon Ó Broin referred to 'Invincible activity in an agrarian
context' in relation to the Loughrea and Barbavilla murders. In an essay on the
'Invincibles' he calls attention to the fact that in July 1885 the attorney general,
Hugh Holmes, prepared notes for Carnarvon, then lord lieutenant, and that
these notes indicated that Fagan and Curley both repeatedly told Mallon of
travelling from Dublin to Kilpatrick to hold a meeting in Fagan's mother's
farmyard where a number of people were sworn into an assassination society
with the object of removing 'local tyrants', one of them being Smythe.[95] It
would appear that such information was given to Mallon in return for their
freedom on certain conditions which were not acceptable to the crown.[96]
Ó Broin speculates that one of the conditions may have been that 'they should
not be asked to name or implicate any person who might be prejudiced by
what they had to communicate'.[97] Incidentally, a strong local tradition which
casts Fagan as an informer has persisted in Collinstown to this day.[98] Thus in
spite of Curry's repudiation of an Invincible link, other sources would indicate
the contrary. It would seem likely that the police had some knowledge of a
meeting which took place in Fagan's, but had received skeletal information
regarding this, and had to depend upon their own resourcefulness to detect
the identity of the conspirators.[99]

Although Curry was dismissive of any connection with the Invincibles –
as it weakened his case to acknowledge a link between the murder and a secret
society – other sources confirm that there was a link with this group. Likewise
they suggest that a meeting did take place in Fagan's yard at which a conspiracy to murder Smythe was developed. Given the several discrepancies
which characterise the McKeons' evidence, it is highly unlikely that these two
witnesses attended this or indeed any other meeting. Although other political
considerations influenced the prospects of having the case reopened, the link
with the Invincibles was ultimately the deciding factor which ensured that the
case remained closed.

Conclusion

Outwardly, the Barbavilla murder was one of the many murders which took place during the land war (1879–82) and was perpetrated in response to an eviction which occurred in the locality. However, this study has found that by examining various aspects of the tenant community in the context of the land war, a more complex picture of the Barbavilla murder emerges. This broader context played a significant role in shaping the events which took place before and after the murder in the parish of Collinstown during 1882. It could be argued, for instance, that the eviction might not have taken place at any other time. Had the agricultural depression of the late 1870s followed by the Land League agitation not occurred, it is likely that Smythe and Riggs would have continued as they were. Likewise the murder of Maria Smythe which followed the eviction was an outcome of the land war. Such an extreme action in response to one eviction by a landlord with an overall good reputation would be a highly unlikely occurrence at any other time. The connection with the Invincibles may have been the ultimate factor which precipitated the perpetration of the murder, again making the Barbavilla murder very much a product of its time.

Owing to the significance of Land League activity in this study, this subject was examined in relation to County Westmeath and, more importantly, to the parish of Collinstown. It was demonstrated, for instance that the tensions which characterised the earlier period of unrest between 1869 and 1871, still persisted in the tenant community in the late 1870s and early 1880s. This was largely attributed to the activities of graziers in relation to land tenure and the conflict between this group and the smaller tenants. This long-term tension was undoubtedly an important motivating factor in mobilising tenants in the Collinstown area to become involved in the Land League in the early 1880s. Policies of the league such as 'rent at the point of a bayonet' and the 'no rent manifesto' were implemented by the local branch in Collinstown. Women participated in the Land League agitation through the activities of the Fore branch of the Ladies' Land League. Their action was characterised by attributes which were traditionally associated with the role of women – such as providing relief for evicted tenants – but which also contained a strong political statement.

Reaction to the Barbavilla murder provided useful insights into the attitudes and assumptions of the local tenant community. It was found that the traditional sectors of landlord support such as the Church of Ireland vestry in Collinstown and the pro-establishment county paper, the *Westmeath Guardian*, were vociferous in their condemnation of the murder. The silence of the tenant community in Collinstown was a traditional response to an agrarian outrage.

This could be interpreted not only as an indication of support for the outrage (or the intention of the outrage), but also that tenants were fearful of the consequences for themselves should they decide to condemn the murder or provide any assistance to the police. The documentary sources examined have not revealed the reaction of the Catholic clergy to the murder, apart from the message which the Vatican sent to the *Daily Telegraph* expressing horror at the outrage.[1] Three years later, Smythe was still underlining the fact that there had been no official condemnation of the murder by the Catholic church, either locally or by any individual prelate. In a letter to an unidentified newspaper entitled 'The last three years of Rome rule' he referred to the fact that 'no Roman Catholic priest or bishop denounced the intentions of the Invincibles'.[2]

In the aftermath of the murder, two important changes occurred in the parish of Collinstown: Smythe left Ireland to live in Ilfracombe, Devon, in England, leaving the affairs of the estate to be managed by a feared non-resident land agent, and a group of local men were convicted for conspiring to murder Smythe. Both of these factors had a profound effect on the local community in Collinstown. Firstly, Smythe's departure heralded a new era in landlord-tenant relations. Henceforth the tenants on the Barbavilla estate were obliged to comply with the estate rules and whatever flexibility in landlord-tenant relations they had previously enjoyed did not apply under the new regime. Secondly, information provided by local men in 1883–4 brought about the arrests and eventual conviction of a group of eleven men for conspiracy to murder Smythe. This study demonstrates that the convicted men received support from the local tenant community as evidenced by the prisoners' fund which was aimed at assisting the prisoners' families and the election of one of the prisoners, William McCormack, as a poor law guardian in 1883. The prisoners also received the support of the local Catholic clergy who were responsible for instigating the above fund and later on for spearheading a campaign to have the case reopened.

Agrarian violence was one of the central themes of this study. Westmeath was found to be a county where there existed a long tradition of rural unrest of which the Barbavilla murder bore many of the traditional hallmarks. Of specific relevance was the response of the British administration to the agrarian violence of the land war 1879–82 by introducing coercive legislation. In particular, the Prevention of Crime Act (Ireland) passed in 1882 had an important bearing on the case of the Barbavilla prisoners in a number of ways.[3] It allowed for witnesses to provide information in a private hearing which was the means by which the McKeons gave their information initially. This legislation also provided for the selection of a panel of special jurors and for the trials being held in another county, in this case, Dublin. These measures had been introduced owing to the difficulty experienced by the guardians of law and order in Ireland in detecting and punishing those responsible for agrarian crime during the land war.

In his account of the Phoenix Park murders, Corfe concluded that:

> Hitherto there had been likelihood of murderers going unpunished;
> now the opposite danger threatened, and henceforth in Ireland crime
> must be followed by punishment even if there were sometimes
> difficulties in finding adequate proof of the guilt of the accused.[4]

In the case of the Barbavilla prisoners, the crime was followed by punishment
in circumstances where the evidence against the accused was open to question.
In this respect, it was similar to a number of other murder cases tried under
the Prevention of Crimes Act (Ireland) such as the Maamtrasna murders and
the Dromulton murder.[5] The attempt made by Rev. John Curry (1846–1912),
parish priest of Collinstown, to have the case reopened in 1884–5 was
unsuccessful owing to the political conventions of the British government in
relation to investigating cases which had been tried under a different administration, and also because of wider political developments in Westminster
during the year of 1885. The connection between this murder and the
Invincibles was undoubtedly another important factor taken into account by
the British government in considering the case.

   In conclusion, one could assume that the Barbavilla murder was a typical
agrarian murder which characterised late nineteenth-century Ireland. It was
perpetrated in response to local circumstances and shared many characteristics
of other outrages. However, it must be said that although it was similar to other
murders, it was different in one respect in that it was linked with a political
group, the Invincibles, who took advantage of local conditions to further their
own cause, the assassination of local figures whom they perceived as 'tyrants'.
Having said that, there were obviously a number of local men who were
predisposed to the ideology of the Invincibles and were prepared to become
actively involved with this group, although given the very nature of secret
societies, it is difficult to evaluate the exact extent to which the Invincibles were
involved with this murder. Nevertheless, this predisposition is linked with the
underlying problems which characterised the tenant community in Collinstown.
Tensions associated with the conflict between tenants and landlords and small
tenants and graziers which were heightened during the land war created the
conditions for an alternative political group to exploit. Therefore, although the
Barbavilla murder was distinctive in this respect, it cannot be completely
dissociated from the general patterns of agrarian violence which were a feature
of late-nineteenth century Ireland. This study also clearly demonstrates the
obvious value of examining a murder using the techniques and methodologies
of local history. Even though on the face of it, the murder at Barbavilla appears
to be yet another agrarian outrage, this study has illustrated the importance of
viewing incidents such as this one within the local context against the backdrop
of wider developments on a provincial or 'national' level.

Notes

ABBREVIATIONS

C.S.O.R.P.	Chief Secretary's Office Registered Papers
CSO CR	Chief Secretary's Office Correspondence Register
H.C.	House of Commons
I.H.S.	*Irish Historical Studies*
N.A.I.	National Archives of Ireland
N.L.I.	National Library of Ireland

INTRODUCTION

1 Richard Griffith, *General valuation of rateable property in Ireland, counties of Meath and Westmeath, valuation of the several tenements in the union of Castletowndelvin situated in the counties above named* (Dublin, 1854), pp 23–77.

2 *Return of owners of land of an acre and upwards, in the several counties, counties of cities, and counties of towns in Ireland* ... p. 86 [C 1492], H.C. 1876, lxxx.

3 Stephen R. Penny, *Smythe of Barbavilla* (Oxford, 1974), p. 31.

4 Christine Casey and Alistair Rowan, *The buildings of Ireland: north Leinster* (London, 1993), p. 217.

5 *Census of Ireland, 1881, ...* vol i, *province of Leinster*, p. 931 [C 3042], H.C 1881, xcvii.

6 Charles Phythian-Adams, *Society, culture and kinship, 1580–1850* (Leicester, 1993), p. xiii.

7 William Barlow Smythe, *The tale of Westmeath wickedness and woe* (Manchester, 1882), p. 1.

8 John Curry, *The Barbavilla trials and the crimes act in Ireland* (3rd ed., Dublin, 1886).

9 The transcripts were destroyed when the Four Courts were burned in 1922.

10 W. E. Vaughan, *Landlords and tenants in mid-Victorian Ireland* (Oxford, 1994); A.C. Murray, 'Agrarian violence and nationalism in nineteenth century Ireland, the myth of ribbonism' in *Irish Economic and Social History*, xiii (1986), pp 56–73; Charles Townshend, *Political violence in Ireland: government and resistance since 1848* (Oxford, 1983); Virginia Crossman, *Politics, law and order in nineteenth-century Ireland* (Dublin, 1996).

11 David Seth Jones, *Graziers, land reform and political conflict in Ireland* (Washington D.C., 1995).

BETWEEN THE FAMINE AND THE LAND WAR

1 Raymond Gillespie and Gerard Moran, 'Writing local history' in Raymond Gillespie and Gerard Moran (eds), *A various country, essays in Mayo history, 1500–1900* (Westport, 1987), p. 21.

2 Charles Townshend, *Political violence in Ireland: government and resistance since 1848* (Oxford, 1983), p. 15.

3 *Report of the select committee on the state of Ireland*, p. 208, H.C. 1831–2 (677), xvi, evidence of Rev. John Burke, Castlepollard.

4 William Pentland, *To the Right Honourable Wm. E. Gladstone, M.P.* (Mullingar, 1871), p. 2.

5 *Report from the select committee appointed to inquire into the state of Westmeath etc. and the nature of a certain unlawful combination existing therein, together with the proceedings to the committee, minutes of evidence* ... (hereafter *S.C. on Westmeath* (1871)) p. 58, H. C. 1871 (147), xiii.

6 A.C. Murray, 'Agrarian violence and nationalism in nineteenth-century Ireland: the myth of ribbonism' in *Irish Economic and Social History*, xiii (1986), p. 71; see also Tom Garvin, 'Defenders; Ribbonmen and others: underground political networks in pre-famine Ireland', in *Past and Present* no. 96 (1982), pp 128–143.

7 *S.C. on Westmeath (1871)*, p. 115.

8 W. E. Vaughan, *Landlords and tenants in mid-Victorian Ireland* (Oxford, 1994), p. 201.

9 Murray, 'Agrarian violence', p. 71.

10 Virginia Crossman, *Politics, law and order, in nineteenth-century Ireland* (Dublin, 1996), p. 124.

11   *S.C. on Westmeath (1871)*, appendix, pp 184–97.

12   George Campbell, *The Irish land* (Dublin, 1869), p. 6.

13   Letter no. 14460 (N.A.I., Chief Secretary's Office, Library, Threatening letters and notices (photographs), 1869–72, album copies p. 23, photographic copy of threatening letter to Michael Hope, Gartlandstown House, [Co. Westmeath], 5 May 1869).

14   Townshend, *Political violence*, p. 9.

15   Vaughan, *Landlords and tenants in mid-Victorian Ireland*, p. 160.

16   Threatening notice no. 14468, (N.A.I., Chief Secretary's Office, Library, Threatening letters and notices (photographs) 1869–72; album copies, p. 27, photographic copy of threatening notice posted at Collinstown Market House, [Co. Westmeath], 14 Feb. 1869).

17   David Seth Jones, *Graziers, land reform and political conflict in Ireland* (Washington D.C., 1995), p. 1.

18   David Seth Jones, 'The cleavage between graziers and peasants in the land struggle, 1890–1910' in Samuel Clark and J.S. Donnelly, Jr. (eds), *Irish peasants: violence and political unrest, 1780–1914* (Manchester, 1983), p. 396.

19   Raymond Crotty, *Irish agricultural production: its volume and structure* (Cork, 1966), p. 60.

20   Crotty, *Irish agricultural production*, p. 376.

21   Oral testimony records that Hope took over Paddy Horan's holding (a small tenant on his land) and made him steward to compensate. The same source also records that he evicted the Gavigan family and took over their nine acres of land. (transcript of Jane Daly's interview with Paddy Tuite age 78, Feb. 1982 (transcript in possession of Jane Daly, Clondalever, Collinstown, Co. Westmeath)).

22   *S.C. on Westmeath (1871)*, appendix, p. 177.

23   William Pentland, *The times we live in: being a few plain facts, plainly stated, showing the loss to Ireland by emigration* (Mullingar, 1873), p. 5.

24   Crotty, *Irish agricultural production*, p. 42.

25   Jones, *Graziers*, p. 4.

26   Samuel Clark, *Social origins of the land war*, (Princeton, N.J., 1979), p. 151.

27   I am indebted to Tommy and Jane Daly, Clondalever, for this information.

28   Clark, *Social origins*, p. 125.

29   Liam Kennedy, 'Regional specialisation, railway development, and Irish agriculture in the nineteenth century' in J.M Goldstrom and L.A. Clarkson (eds), *Irish population, economy and society* (Oxford, 1981), p. 192.

30   R.V. Comerford, 'Ireland 1850–71: post-famine and mid-Victorian' in W.E. Vaughan

31   (ed.), *A new history of Ireland, v: Ireland under the union, ii (1801–70)* (Oxford, 1989), p. 375. Royal commission of inquiry into primary education (Ireland), vol. vi, educational census, returns showing number of children actually present in each primary school, 25 June 1868, with introductory observations and analytical index, pt v, p. 79 [C 6], H.C. 1870, xxviii, 133.

32   Report of the commissioners appointed to take the census of Ireland for the year 1841, p. 116 [504], H.C. 1843, xxiv; Census of Ireland, 1881, . . . vol. i, province of Leinster, p. 940 [C 3042], H.C. 1881, xcvii.

33   Clark, *Social origins*, p. 123.

34   Comerford, 'Ireland 1850–71', p. 376.

35   Comerford, 'Ireland 1850–71', p. 376.

36   *Westmeath Examiner*, 23 Sept. 1882.

37   James S. Donnelly Jr., *The land and the people of nineteenth century Cork: the rural economy and the land question* (London, 1975), p. 249.

38   *Westmeath Guardian*, 16 May 1850.

39   *Westmeath Guardian*, 16 May 1850.

40   *Westmeath Guardian*, 16 May 1850, 27 May 1852.

41   Clark, *Social origins*, p. 257.

42   The bill to amend the law of tenants' emblements and the tenants' improvements bill (*Westmeath Guardian*, 5 Apr. 1860).

43   For example, *Westmeath Guardian*, 5 Jan. 1860.

44   B. M. Walker, 'The Irish electorate, 1865–1915' in *I.H.S.*, xviii, no. 71 (1973), p. 376.

45   K.T Hoppen, 'Landlords, society and electoral politics in mid-nineteenth century Ireland' in *Past and Present*, no. 75 (1977), p. 92.

46   William Feingold, 'The tenants' movement to capture the poor law boards, 1877–1886' in *Albion*, vii (1975), pp 216–31.

47   R.V. Comerford, 'Patriotism as pastime: the appeal of fenianism in the mid-1860s' in *I.H.S.*, xxii, no. 87 (1981), p. 242.

48   Brian Griffin, 'The I.R.B. in Connacht and Leinster, 1858–1878' unpublished M.A. thesis, St Patrick's College, Maynooth, 1983, p. 64.

49   Maurice Johnson, 'The Fenian amnesty movement' unpublished M.A. thesis, St Patrick's College Maynooth, 1980, p. 549.

50   Griffin, 'The I.R.B', pp 47, 106.

51   John Curry, *The Barbavilla trials and the crimes act in Ireland* (3rd ed., Dublin, 1886) p. 40.

52   B files, no. 134 (N.A.I., Chief Secretary's Office, B files 1880–3, 3/716) .

53   Interview with Peter Nolan, grandson of Pat Fitzsimons, 14 Aug. 1990; *Meath Chronicle* 13 Oct. 1934.

54   B files, no. 249 (N.A.I., Chief Secretary's Office, B files 1880–3, 3/716).

THE LAND WAR

1   *Preliminary report from her majesty's commissioners on agriculture*, p. 871 [C 2778], H.C. 1881, xv.

2   *Agricultural statistics of Ireland for the year 1879*, p. 71 [C 2534], H.C. 1880, lxxvi, 885.

3   Central Statistics Office, *Farming since the famine: Irish historical statistics, 1847–1996* (Dublin, 1997), p. 200.

4   Between March and September it rained 125 out of 183 days (J.E. Doherty and D.J. Hickey, *A chronology of Irish history since 1500* (Dublin, 1989), p. 153).

5   *Agricultural statistics . . . 1879*, p. 71 [C 2534], H.C. 1880, lxxvi, 885.

6   *Agricultural statistics . . . 1879*, p. 61 [C 2534], H.C. 1880, lxxvi, 874; *Agricultural statistics . . . 1880*, p. 59 [C 2932], H.C. 1881, xcii, 743.

7   Samuel Clark, *Social origins of the land war* (Princeton, N.J.,1979) p. 228.

8   *Westmeath Guardian*, 3 Oct. 1879.

9   *Returns of numbers in receipt of relief in the several unions in Ireland on the 1st day of January, the 1st day of March and the 1st day of June in 1878, 1879 and 1880*, p. 9, H.C. 1880 (420–sess. 2), lxii, 297.

10   *Westmeath Guardian*, 12 Sept. 1879.

11   Clark, *Social origins*, p. 232.

12   Smyth of Drumcree rental 1871– 1900 (MS in the possession of Billy Smyth, Drumcree, Collinstown, County Westmeath)

13   W.E.Vaughan, *Landlords and tenants in mid-Victorian Ireland* (Oxford, 1994), p. 243.

14   William Barlow Smythe, *The Tale of Westmeath wickedness and woe* (Manchester, 1882), p. 8.

15   Smythe, *Tale of Westmeath*, p.8.

16   *Westmeath Guardian*, 10 Oct. 1881.

17   *Westmeath Guardian*, 2 Dec. 1881; Howard Bury papers (Westmeath County Library, K/8/M).

18   Clark, *Social origins*, p. 236.

19   Clark, *Social origins*, pp 246–9.

20   Clark, *Social origins*, p. 303.

21   Clark, *Social origins*, p. 303.

22   Clark, *Social origins*, p. 302.

23   Norman Dunbar Palmer, *The Irish land league crisis* (New Haven, CT., 1940), p. 136.

24   Charles Townshend, *Political violence in Ireland: government and resistance since 1848* (Oxford, 1983), p. 115.

25   *Returns for each month of the years 1879 and 1880, of the number of Land league meetings held and agrarian crimes reported to Inspector-General of the Royal Irish Constabulary in each county* p. 2, H.C. 1881 (5), lxxvii, 794 [hereafter *L.L. meetings 1879–80*]

26   *Nation*, 3 Apr. 1880.

27   Clark, *Social origins*, p. 280.

28   Smythe, *The Tale of Westmeath*, p. 26.

29   File for application for legal aid from Collinstown Fore branch, 3 July 1881 (N.L.I., Land League papers, MS 17710 (7)).

30   *Westmeath Guardian*, 6 July 1883.

31   *Nation*, 23 Apr. 1881; Richard Griffith, *General valuation of rateable property in Ireland: counties of Meath and Westmeath, valuation of the several tenements in the union of Castletoundelvin situated in the counties above named* (Dublin, 1854), p. 76.

32   Clark, *Social origins*, p. 301.

33   *Westmeath Guardian*, 24 Dec. 1880.

34   Clark, *Social origins*, p. 290.

35   *Westmeath Guardian*, 5 Nov. 1880.

36   *Westmeath Guardian*, 24 Dec. 1880.

37   *Weekly Freeman*, 8 Jan. 1881.

38   *Nation*, 19 June 1880.

39   *Nation*, 3 Apr. 1880.

40   *Weekly Freeman*, 8 Jan. 1881.

41   *Westmeath Guardian*, 24 Dec. 1880.

42   For the Killough meeting, for instance, the two M.P.s were brought in a brake from the railway station to O'Callaghan's 'establishment' in Killucan and entertained before the meeting. From there they were accompanied 'by a long line of jaunting cars and pedestrians, wearing green sashes and carrying long white staves' (*Westmeath Guardian*, 5 Nov. 1880).

43   *L.L. meetings 1879–80*, p. 4.

44   *Returns by provinces of agrarian offences throughout Ireland reported to Inspector-General of Royal Irish Constabulary between the 1st day of January 1881 and the 31st day of December, 1881*, p 6, H.C. 1882 (72), lv, 22 [hereafter *Agrarian offences, 1881*].

45   *L.L. meetings 1879–80*, pp 2–3; *Agrarian offences, 1881*, pp 6–7.

46   *Westmeath Guardian*, 30 Dec. 1881.

47   Clark, *Social origins*, p. 320.

48   *Westmeath Guardian*, 24 Dec. 1880.

49   Paul Bew, *Land and the national question in Ireland, 1858–82* (Dublin, 1978), p. 238.

50   *Westmeath Guardian*, 24 Dec. 1880; Nolan, who became a poor law guardian in Mullingar Union, was very active in the Land League in Westmeath and was also involved in the Labourers' League.

51   *Nation*, 23 Apr. 1881.

52   Clark, *Social origins*, p. 301.

53   Clark, *Social origins*, p. 302.

54   *Nation*, 10 Sept. 1881.

55   J.W. H. Carter, *The land war and its leaders in Queen's County, 1879–82* (Portlaoise, 1994), p. 176.

56   Jane McL. Côté, *Fanny and Anna Parnell: Ireland's patriot sisters* (Dublin, 1991), p. 180.

57   Côté, *Fanny and Anna Parnell*, p. 153.

58   *Nation*, 23 Apr. 1881.

59   Land League application form for legal costs from the Collinstown Fore branch, 3

July 1881 (N.L.I., Land League papers, MS 17710 (7)).

60   Côté, *Fanny and Anna Parnell*, p. 158.

61   Côté, *Fanny and Anna Parnell*, p. 153.

62   D.B. Cashman, *Life of Michael Davitt, founder of the National Land League* (London, 1882), p. 231.

63   *Freeman's Journal*, 12 Mar. 1881.

64   Jane K. TeBrake, 'Irish peasant women in revolt: the Land League years' in *I.H.S.*, xxviii, no. 109 (1992), p. 70.

65   Records of the commissioners of national education, Collinstown National School (N.A.I., ED 9/2477, 1884).

66   Other members mentioned in the *Nation* were the two Miss O'Reillys, the two Miss Fagans the two Miss Cullens, Miss Smyth, Miss Halpin and Miss Dargan (*Nation*, 11 Mar. 1882).

67   Records of the commissioners of national education, Collinstown National School (N.A.I., ED 9/2477, 1884).

68   Mary Cantwell's husband Edward, a farmer and auctioneer living in Gilliardstown, was listed as one of the dignitaries on the platform at the demonstration meeting in Castlepollard on 2 January 1880.

69   *Nation*, 11 Mar. 1882.

70   *Nation*, 18 Feb. 1882.

71   *Freeman's Journal*, 6 Apr. 1882.

72   Virginia Crossman, *Politics, law and order in nineteenth-century Ireland* (Dublin, 1996), p. 143.

73   *United Ireland*, 22 July 1882.

74   *Nation*, 28 Jan. 1882 ; this was Peter Fagan, the fenian from Bennison Lodge referred to in chapter one, who was in custody in Enniskillen jail from 9 January until 25 March, 1882 (*Protection of persons and property act 1881: list of all persons detained in prison under the statute 44 Vict., c.4, to the end of March 1882*, p.6 H.C. 1883 (156), lv, 649.)

75   *Nation*, 20 May 1882.

76   McL. Côté, *Fanny and Anna Parnell*, p. 199.

77   T.W. Moody, *Davitt and Irish revolution, 1846–82* (Oxford 1982), p. 494.

78   The farm in question was owned by the trustees of Wilson's Hospital, Multyfarnham, and the annual rent was £85 (*Daily Express*, 11 June 1884).

79   *Daily Express*, 10 June 1884.

80   Extract from 'W.B. Smythe Esq. Barbavilla' Stephen R. Penny, *Smythe of Barbavilla* (Oxford, 1974), p. 117.

81   *Return of owners of land of an acre and upwards in the several counties, counties of cities, and counties of towns in Ireland* . . . p. 86, [C 1492], H.C. 1876, lxxx.

82   Smythe, *The Tale of Westmeath*, p. 22.

83   Smythe, *The Tale of Westmeath*, p. 6.

84   *Westmeath Guardian*, 7 Apr. 1882.

85   *Westmeath Guardian*, 1 June–5 Aug. 1852.

86   *Westmeath Guardian*, 5 Aug. 1852; see also J. H. Whyte, 'The influnce of Catholic clergy on elections in nineteenth century Ireland' in *English Historical Review*, lxxv (1960), pp 239–59.

87   *Westmeath Guardian*, 15 Jan. 1863.

88   In a letter written in the *Westmeath Guardian*, 2 Dec. 1881, Smythe reacted strongly to the leading article in the *Westmeath Guardian*, 25 Nov. 1881, which advocated that the tenants flock to the land court.

89   *Westmeath Guardian*, 1 Oct. 1880.

'ANOTHER SHOCKING MURDER IN WESTMEATH'

1   This was the title of the article about the murder in the *Westmeath Guardian*, 2 Apr. 1882.

2   William Barlow Smythe, *The tale of Westmeath, wickedness and woe* (Manchester, 1882) p. 3.

3   Letter from Smythe to E. Brice, 14 Apr. 1882 (Westmeath County Library, Smythe papers).

4   William Barlow Smythe, *Tale of Westmeath*, p. 3.

5   Interview with Peter Nolan, Glenidan, 14 Aug. 1990; taped interviews with Paddy Tuite, Rickardstown, age 94, 13 Dec. 1996 and 11 Jan. 1997 (tape in possession of writer).

6   Tuite interview, 13 Dec. 1996.

7   Letter from Smythe to chief secretary, 28 May 1883 (N.A.I., C.S.O.R.P. 1883/13096).

8   Smythe, *The tale of Westmeath*, p. 3.

9   Smythe, *The tale of Westmeath*, p. 7.

10   Smythe, *The tale of Westmeath*, p. 4.

11   The tenant in question was Joseph Fagan, who had a holding of 145.25 statute acres at a rent of £142. At this stage, Smythe had Fagan's improvements valued which came to between £300 and £400. Approximately half of this amount was used to 'liquidate the arrears' and the remainder was paid to Fagan in cash (Privately published leaflet giving the facts of the case of Fagan, Westmeath County Library, Smythe papers).

12   The sectarian slant to the affair has interestingly survived in folklore (see Joseph Wade's notes, Westmeath County Library).

13   Smythe, *The tale of Westmeath*, p. 28.

14   Smythe, *The tale of Westmeath*, p. 5.

15   Smythe, *The tale of Westmeath*, p. 6.

16   Smythe, *The tale of Westmeath*, p. 6. Viscount Mountmorres was murdered near Clonbur, County Galway on 25 September 1880.

17   Smythe, *The tale of Westmeath*, p. 7.

18   Smythe, *The tale of Westmeath*, p. 6.

19 Smythe, *The tale of Westmeath*, p. 26.
20 Smythe, *The tale of Westmeath*.
21 Smythe, *The tale of Westmeath*.
22 He had held the position of agent for approximately 30 years (*Westmeath Examiner*, 21 June 1884).
23 One case was on 7 June 1881, which resulted in his being fined 5 shillings (25p).
24 Smythe, *The tale of Westmeath*, p. 9.
25 Smythe to chief secretary, 19 Nov. 1881 (N.A.I., Country Letter Book, CSO LB 45)
26 Letters from the chief secretary's office, Nov.–Mar. 1882 (N.A.I., Country letter book, CSO LB 45)
27 Smythe, *The tale of Westmeath*, p. 4.
28 Smythe, *The tale of Westmeath*, p. 4.
29 *Westmeath Guardian*, 25 Mar. 1882.
30 Smythe, *The tale of Westmeath*, p. 10 (this letter is reproduced in its original form). Crawford, an agent who resided in the Clonmellon area, was shot coming home from church on 19 March 1882 (*Freeman's Journal*, 20 Mar. 1882).
31 Smythe, *The tale of Westmeath*, p. 4.
32 The sister of Smythe's wife, Emily, who had died in 1837.
33 *Westmeath Guardian*, 7 Apr. 1882.
34 Smythe, *The tale of Westmeath*, p. 25.
35 Smythe, *The tale of Westmeath*, p. 29.
36 Smythe, *The tale of Westmeath*, p. 29: the phrase 'force is no remedy' was first used by John Bright and came to epitomise the apparent reluctance on the part of the Liberals to pass coercive legislation in Ireland at this time.
37 Smythe to Gladstone, 3 May 1884 (Westmeath County Library, Smythe papers).
38 *Westmeath Guardian*, 7 Apr. 1882.
39 Smythe, *The tale of Westmeath*, p. 23.
40 Elizabeth Batt, *The Moncks and Charleville House* (Cork, 1979), p. 259.
41 *Westmeath Examiner*, 14 Apr. 1882.
42 Smythe, *The tale of Westmeath*, p. 32.
43 *Westmeath Guardian*, 14 Apr. 1882.
44 *Daily Express*, 19 Apr. 1882.
45 *Florence Arnold-Forster, Florence Arnold Forster's Irish Journal*, (eds.) T.W. Moody and R.A.J. Hawkins with Margaret Moody (Oxford, 1988), p. 433.
46 *Nation*, 8 Apr. 1882.
47 *Freeman's Journal*, 4 Apr. 1882.
48 Smythe, *The tale of Westmeath*, p. 30.
49 *Nation*, 8 Apr. 1882.
50 Smythe, *The tale of Westmeath*, p. 28.
51 Smythe, *The tale of Westmeath*, p. 23.
52 *Westmeath Guardian*, 11 Aug. 1882.
53 Smythe, *The tale of Westmeath*, p. 23. Riggs was still in custody in June 1882, but eventually was released. (Report from

Captain Butler, 8 June 1882 (N.A.I., C.S.O.R.P. 1882/36107).
54 Curry, *Barbavilla Trials*, p. xiii.
55 Luke Farrelly died in April 1884 and was replaced by John Curry in May 1884.
56 This will be examined in more detail in the following chapter.
57 *Westmeath Guardian*, 9 June 1882.
58 Jane McL. Côté, *Fanny and Anna Parnell, Ireland's patriot sisters* (Dublin, 1991), p. 203.
59 Unidentified newspaper cutting from Smythe's album, 14 July 1882 (Westmeath County Library, Smythe papers).
60 Captain Butler to chief secretary, 21 Oct. 1882 (N.A.I., C.S.O.R.P., 1883/13096).
61 Law adviser to Captain Butler, 26 Oct. 1882 (N.A.I., C.S.O.R.P., 1883/13096).
62 Smythe to chief secretary, 26 May 1883 (N.A.I., C.S.O.R.P. 1883/13096).
63 Captain Butler to chief secretary 31 May 1883 (N.A.I., C.S.O.R.P. 1883/13096).

THE AFTERMATH OF THE MURDER

1   *Westmeath Guardian* 14 Apr. 1882; of the first six men initially arrested Gill and Fagan were discharged, but the others were remanded in custody for eight days.
2   He is not named but most likely was Sergeant Lynch.
3   Taped interview with Paddy Tuite, age 94, Rickardstown, 13 Dec. 1996 (tape in possession of writer).
4   Report from Captain Butler, special resident magistrate to chief secretary, 8 June 1882 (N.A.I., C.S.O.R.P. 1882/36107).
5   Report from Captain Butler, 8 June 1882 (N.A.I., C.S.O.R.P. 1882/36107).
6   Report from Captain Butler, 8 June 1882 (N.A.I., C.S.O.R.P. 1882/ 36107).
7   According to Paddy Tuite, Boyhan was given £3 – the fare for travelling to the United States – by a local woman, Ellen Keenan, who had a small shop (Tuite interview).
8   *Westmeath Examiner*, 7 Apr. 1883.
9   *Westmeath Examiner*, 5 May 1883.
10 *Daily Express*, 24 Apr. 1884.
11 John Curry, *The Barbavilla trials and the crimes act in Ireland* (3rd ed., Dublin, 1886), p. 16.
12 Curry, *The Barbavilla trials*, p. 17.
13 *Westmeath Guardian*, 10 Dec. 1883.
14 The three depositions are given in full in Curry, *The Barbavilla trials*, pp 61–2.
15 Curry, *The Barbavilla trials*, p. 61.
16 Curry, *The Barbavilla trials*, p. 61.
17 Curry, *The Barbavilla trials*, p. 8.
18 Edward Carson, then a young barrister, was a member of the defending counsel. He stated in his summary that if the evidence of the McKeons was to be taken seriously,

it meant that that 'the crown had discredited their own evidence by not charging Elliott with the capital offence'. (*Daily Express*, 12 Dec. 1883).

19 *Daily Express*, 24 Apr. 1884. An incident which occurred in Dublin on 21 April 1884, two days earlier may have had some impact on the outcome of this trial. Sheets of mourning paper with 'God save Ireland' written on them and with green ribbons attached were left in the Phoenix Park on the spot where Cavendish and Burke had been murdered the previous year and outside the home of Chief Justice Palles in Fitzwilliam Place.

20 *Westmeath Guardian*, 22 June 1883.

21 The three people were: Edward McCaffrey, known as E. Mack, Daniel Curley, and Michael Fagan.

22 John Fagan left in August 1882 (*Westmeath Guardian*, 20 July 1883).

23 This was Joseph McGrath who had died of scarlet fever in May 1882.

24 Curry, *The Barbavilla trials*, p. 19.

25 Tom Corfe, *The Phoenix park murder: conflict, compromise and tragedy in Ireland, 1879–1882* (London, 1968), p. 242.

26 Curry, *The Barbavilla trials*, pp 38–9.

27 Curry, *The Barbavilla trials*, p. xii.

28 Curry, *The Barbavilla trials*, p. xiii.

29 Curry, *The Barbavilla trials*, p. xiii.

30 Curry, *The Barbavilla trials*, p. xii.

31 Curry, *The Barbavilla trials*, p. xii.

32 *Daily Express*, 22 April 1884.

33 *Westmeath Guardian*, 6 July 1883.

34 *Irish Times*, 12 July 1883.

35 Unidentified newspaper cutting regarding trial, 23 Apr. 1884 (Westmeath County Library, Smythe papers).

36 Unidentified newspaper cutting regarding trial, 23 Apr. 1884.

37 Unidentified newspaper cutting regarding trial, 23 Apr. 1884.

38 Curry, *The Barbavilla Trials*, p. 3.

39 *Daily Express*, 9 June 1884; McKeon denied this at the trials.

40 Curry, *The Barbavilla Trials*, p. 82.

41 *Westmeath Examiner*, 26 July 1883.

42 *Westmeath Examiner*, 26 July 1883.

43 *Weekly Freeman*, 7 July 1883.

44 *Westmeath Examiner*, 14 July 1883. Each donated 10 shillings (50p) which was listed with a subscription from Edward Cantwell of Gilliardstown for the same amount.

45 *Westmeath Examiner*, 8 Sept. 1883.

46 *Westmeath Examiner*, 8 Sept. 1883.

47 *Westmeath Examiner*, 8 Sept. 1883.

48 *Westmeath Examiner*, 11 Aug. 1883.

49 William and Robert McCormack were first cousins.

50 *Westmeath Examiner*, 16 Nov. 1883.

51 William F. Feingold, 'The tenants movement to capture the Irish poor law boards, 1877–1886' in Alan O'Day (ed.) *Reactions to nationalism* (London, 1987), p. 93 (first published in *Albion*, vii, no. 3 (1975), pp 216–31).

52 *Westmeath Examiner*, 14 June 1881.

53 Cole was the second 'approver', the first being Pat Hanlon.

54 Curry, *The Barbavilla Trials*, p. 42.

55 At the trials on 11 June (after Cole had become an approver), R.I.C. Sergeant Humphrey Tilson deposed that William Woods was not and never had been in police custody. However, he believed Woods was involved in the conspiracy but there had not been sufficient evidence to warrant his arrest (unidentified newspaper cutting, June 1884 (Westmeath County Library, Smythe papers)). On hearing that his name had been mentioned in court, Fitzsimons sailed for the United States. When he arrived in New York he made an unsuccessful attempt to have a subscription opened for the Barbavilla prisoners in the *Irish World*. He remained in the United States for approximately three years before returning to Ireland (*Meath Chronicle*, 13 Oct.1934; article written by his son-in-law, Christopher Nolan.)

56 He claimed in his statement that Riggs was an old member of the fenian society, a fact which has not been substantiated by any other source examined to date.

57 Curry, *The Barbavilla trials*, p. 42.

58 Curry, *The Barbavilla trials*, p. 7.

59 *Daily Express*, 23 June 1884.

60 Virginia Crossman, *Politics, law and order in nineteenth-century Ireland* (Dublin, 1996), p. 224.

61 Jarlath Waldron, *Maamtrasna: the murders and the mystery* (Dublin, 1992).

62 *Freeman's Journal*, 14 Feb. 1884.

63 *Daily Express*, 12 June 1884; Rebecca McCormack was not the officially appointed treasurer as such, but collected subscriptions for the Ladies' Land League in the Collinstown end of the parish.

64 *Daily Express*, 10 June 1884.

65 Crossman, *Politics, law and order*, p. 143.

66 J.L. Hammond, *Gladstone and the Irish nation* (London, 1938), p. 326.

67 Expenses of Property Defence men on farm of P.Cole, Aug. 1884 (N.A.I., CSO CR 188 1884 index).

68 Curry, *The Barbavilla trials*, p. 2. In spite of the fact that Cole came forward, according to a local source he never fully succeeded in reintegrating with the community and he and his family eventually moved to Belfast

(Joseph Wade's notes, Westmeath County Library).

69 This time it was in the presence of three priests (Curry, *The Barbavilla trials*, p. 2).

70 Curry, *The Barbavilla trials*, p. 3.

71 Curry, *The Barbavilla trials*, p. 3.

72 Curry, *The Barbavilla trials*, p. 5.

73 Curry, *The Barbavilla trials*, p. 5

74 Curry, *The Barbavilla trials*, preface to the first edition.

75 *Westmeath Examiner*, 25 July. 1885.

76 *Nation*, 25 July 1885.

77 Alan O'Day, *Parnell and the first home rule episode* (Dublin, 1986), p. 43.

78 R.V. Comerford, 'Parnell era, 1883–91' in W.E. Vaughan (ed.), *A new history of Ireland , vi: Ireland under the union*, ii (1870–1921) (Oxford, 1996), p. 60.

79 *Nation*, 25 July 1883.

80 Curry, *The Barbavilla trials*, p. vi.

81 *Westmeath Examiner*, 5 Sept. 1885.

82 Curry, *The Barbavilla trials*, p. vii.

83 Curry, *The Barbavilla trials*, p. viii.

84 Curry, *The Barbavilla trials*, p. ix.

85 In addition to the account book, there was the evidence of witness John Mahon, a baker who was working in Brogan's at that time. He testified at the trials that he saw McKeon senior in Brogan's on the evening the meeting was alleged to have taken place. The bakehouse was being re-floored at the time and McKeon was engaged in the work. He conversed with him in the shop at about half past eight when McKeon was 'somewhat under the influence of drink' (*Daily Express*, 13 Dec. 1883).

86 Curry, *The Barbavilla trials*, p. ix.

87 *Westmeath Examiner*, 17 Oct. 1885.

88 Curry, *The Barbavilla trials*, p. xiv.

89 Curry, *The Barbavilla trials*, p. xiv.

90 *Lloyd's Weekly News*, 25 July 1909 (N.L.I., Ó Broin Papers, MS 24893).

91 Lord Eversley, *Gladstone and Ireland* (London, 1910), p. 183.

92 Frederick Moir Bussy, *Irish conspiracies: recollection of John Mallon (the great Irish detective) and other reminiscences* (London and Glasgow, 1912), p. 132.

93 Bussy, *Irish conspiracies*, p. 132.

94 Bussy, *Irish conspiracies*, p. 122.

95 Leon Ó Broin, 'The Invincibles' in T. Desmond Williams (ed.), *Secret societies in Ireland* (Dublin, 1973), p. 123.

96 Ó Broin, 'The Invincibles', p. 123.

97 Ó Broin, 'The Invincibles', p. 123.

98 Fagan was in arrested on 20 January 1883. His trial took place on 25–6 April 1883. It was during the month of April the Barbavilla murder investigation began to make progress.

99 Another link between the Barbavilla murder and the Invincibles was the 'Paris letters', documents which were found in the possession of Fred Allan, a journalist with the *Freeman's Journal* who was involved with the Irish Republican Brotherhood. They had come into the hands of the police through the 'dead letter' office in Paris, and were said to contain references to people who were involved in the Phoenix Park murders and the Barbavilla murder (Leon O Broin, *Revolutionary underground: the story of the Irish Republican Brotherhood, 1858–1924* (Dublin, 1976), p. 37). Allan was acquitted because it could not be conclusively proven that he wrote the letters (see the *Irishman*, 8 Nov.–13 Dec. 1884).

CONCLUSION

1 *Nation*, 8 Apr. 1882.

2 Unidentified newspaper cutting, 1885 (Westmeath County Library, Smythe papers).

3 Prevention of Crime (Ireland) Act, 45 & 46 Vict. c.25.

4 Tom Corfe, *The Phoenix park murders: conflict, compromise and tragedy in Ireland, 1879–1882* (London, 1968), p. 68.

5 Jarlath Waldron, *Maamtrasna: the murders and the mystery* (Dublin, 1992); Peter O' Sullivan, 'Murder at Dromulton, an incident in the land war in Kerry' Unpublished M.A. thesis, St. Patrick's College, Maynooth, 1996.